Jainism As Metaphilosophy

Sri Garib Dass Oriental Series-No. 120

Jainism As Metaphilosophy

S. GOPALAN
Department of Philosophy
National University of Singapore

SRI SATGURU PUBLICATIONS
A Division of
INDIAN BOOKS CENTRE
DELHI INDIA

Published by :

SRI SATGURU PUBLICATIONS,
Indological & Oriental Publishers,
a Division of
Indian Books Centre,
40/5, Shakti Nagar,
Delhi–110007
India

First Edition : Delhi 1991

ISBN 81–7030–265–X

Printed at:
D. K. Fine Art Press, Delhi.

Printed in India

CONTENTS

PREFACE

The theme of the present work suggested itself to me as I was working on the two lectures "Philosophical Perspectives of Jainism" I was invited to deliver in November, 1986 by the University of Madras. I felt honoured indeed by the invitation since the prestigious Mahasati Tarabaiswamy Endowment Lectureship of Jaina Philosophy was instituted only during 1983-84 and I was the third one to be called upon to give my philosophical perceptions on this ancient Indian tradition!

The task was an onerous one, for it is not easy to disentangle the philosophical aspects of the Jaina tradition from its religious aspects. Though this is a characteristic of the Indian tradition as a whole, the enormous amount of misunderstanding that surrounds Jainism in general and the doctrines of *Anekāntavāda*, *Nayavāda* and *Syādvāda* in particular, makes the philosophical treatment of the latter especially hazarduous. For this very reason I chose the contemporary theme of *meta-philosophy* as my frame of reference.

In this study I have attempted to illustrate that by deliberately asking questions like: "What is the scope and subject-matter of Philosophy?" and "How should philosophers proceed in their analyses of rival systems of thought?" one can better appreciate the deeper philosophical import of Jainism.

After spelling out the idea of metaphilosophy as I see it, I have argued that a constructive-critical approach to sister-systems is exhorted by Jainism as a great responsibility of philosophy. I have also tried to indicate that though the doctrinal aspects of philosophy are *distinguishable* from its methodological aspects, they are not distinct. I have been selective in regard to the rich material available on Jainism to spotlight the issues involved.

I must record here my thanks to the Donors of the Jaina Lectureship and to my former teacher, Professor R. Balasubramanian, ex-Director of the Dr S. Radhakrishnan Institute for Advanced Study in Philosophy,

University of Madras, for having mooted the idea that I should give a thought to the Jaina of concept of philosophy in the lectures.

January 23, 1991
Department of Philosophy
National University of Singapore

S. GOPALAN

Chapter One
PRELIMINARY CONSIDERATIONS

For those accustomed to inquiring into the significance of the various humanistic studies like economics, sociology and political science (which have today become autonomous, having branched off from their mother-discipline, *philosophy*) asking the following questions seems vitally important: (i) What precisely is their scope? (ii) How can their subject-matter be defined? and (iii) Why do they adopt certain methods which characterise them? It seems paradoxical indeed that even after centuries of exitence of these disciplines, such questions are still being asked. What is even more perplexing is that there is no agreement amongst scholars of any one discipline in regard to the way its scope and subject-matter are to be indicated. A serious student cannot help reflecting about the situation, - particularly since these disciplines have, during their own course of development, been dividing themselves into different 'schools'. What is particularly interesting and significant is that these different 'schools' (of sociology, economics, etc.), on analysis, reveal different *concepts* of the disciplines underlying them.

The case is not different with philosophy which gave them birth. Here too different definitions have been proposed and are continuing to be proposed, but with no prospects of agreement amongst philosophers anywhere in sight. In regard to the areas which need to be explored and also on the question of the methods of investigation, hot debates have been witnessed. Whether the reference is to the ancient, medieval or modern times, lack of agreement rather than consensus among scholars, characterises the situation. Add to that the fact that western and Indian conceptions of philosophy show even more marked differences, the difficulties involved in spelling out the general scope of the subject become clearer still.

Whatever may be the reasons for such sharp and unreconciled (possibly irreconcilable) differences between philosophers, one thing is clear. Reconsidering the idea of philosophy from as many angles as it has been done, is still deemed necessary and important. This might perhaps be justification enough for reconsidering the task, the subject-matter and methodology of philosophy.

It might warrant, more specifically, our undertaking to reinterpret the scope of philosophy as envisaged in the Jaina tradition; for, to say the least, the Jaina conception of philosophy has often been subjected to grave misunderstanding. One other important reason for our considering it worthwhile delineating the Jaina perspective may be indicated. The Jaina tradition which has been part and parcel of Indian thought from its early beginnings, is found on analysis, to incorporate within itself, a deliberate attempt at suggesting as to how to do philosophy. By this is not meant that a concept of philosophy is not discernible in the other schools of thought within the Indian philosophical tradition. What is rather suggested is that amongst all systems of Indian thought, Jainism is seen to have addressed itself specifically to the question: "How should philosophical systems proceed in analysing their subject-matter and arriving at philosophical positions?" Since Jainism, in addition to proposing its own doctrines and theories (as other systems of philosophy do) is seen to be greatly concerned with the issue just indicated, it could be regarded both as a system of philosophy and as metaphilosophy.

Despite the fact that Jainism has its own distinguishing features and has its own distinct and rich contribution to make and distinctive characteristics, it ought not to be looked upon as representing a totally independent stream of thought. For, the doctrines which are characterised today as Jaina, had their origins in the hoary past of the Indian tradition. The early beginnings of Indian philosophy have hence to be reconsidered and pondered over again. This is with a view to emphasising that notwithstanding the differences in the viewpoints discernible in the three major traditions of Indian thought, the dominant motif of the latter found expression in divergent ways in and through the different streams representing Hinduism, Jainism and Buddhism. Researches by eminent scholars have clearly brought out the point that the three traditions of

India were, especially in their formative phases, indistinguishable from one another.

Sometimes it is suggested that they are understandable only in terms of the earliest phase of the Indian tradition, now referred to as Brahmanism. But it should be pointed out here that the difficulties encountered in the conceptualisation of Brahmanism would go to show that a stage even previous to Brahmanism should be visualised.[1] For, by considering the post-Vedic era (which exhibits the growth of religious and philosophical ideas under the overarching authority of the Veda) also as Brahmanism and considering Manu Dharma-*Śāstra* as representing classical Brahmanism, the earlier phase which contained germinal ideas for Jainism tends to be glossed over.

The earlier stage of development of Indian thought, the pre-Brahmanical, may be referred to as the proto-Hindu phase. This may be visualised as containing a world of ideas which provided the soil and grist for the development of Hinduism, Jainism and Buddhism later on. In this connection, R. Weiler's reference to the early Indian tradition is topically valuable. He observes:

> Brahmanism, while not necessarily representing the most ancient religion of the Indian sub-continent, is that system of belief and ritual practice to which Indians have historically looked back as the source of their religious traditions. Whether in later Hinduism which tenaciously holds to much of the Brahmanical tradition, or in Buddhism which rejects much of it, there is presupposed this highly conscious and articulate cult, the central feature of a way of life made known through the ages by the earliest body of formal literature, the Veda. Though it is difficult to establish definite continuity in the development of religious ideas in India dating from the Indus Valley civilisation to modern times, it is however possible to distinguish a clearly non-Aryan (which may or may not be pre-Aryan) source for many of the concepts which characterise that religion ... known as 'Hinduism' in India today.[2]

It might be obvious from the above that I am not introducing here a term which is more acceptable and less-loaded for merely getting over the difficulties involved in conceptualising Brahmanism. What I am suggesting is that since the terms *Brahmanism* and *Hinduism*[3] have acquired vast meanings, thanks to the painstaking researches by scholars, the usage of those terms have quite often to be delimited to particular phases of the development of Indian thought while discussing specific issues. It is indeed symptomatic of a curious situation that while the research-findings referred to just now are valuable in indicating that extreme caution is to be observed while using the terms to explain the development of Indian thought, they are by themselves less helpful for an unambiguous appreciation of the fact that there was an earlier phase of development of Indian thought when perhaps ideas, especially on basic issues and concepts, co-existed, and there was also a freer flow and a more whole-hearted acceptance of certain ideas from different sources.

Wilfred Cantwell Smith is quite appreciative of this aspect, and in clear and unambiguous language, he throws valuable light on the whole issue of the three traditions. He writes :

> That the Buddhist and Jain communities constituted separate religions outside, rather than particular movements within the total complex of 'Hinduism' is, I would hold, impossible to maintain with either historical or logical consistency. One would hardly even attempt it except from purely arbitrary or anyway purely modern premises. By formulating this sentence on the basis of 'communities' I have taken sides on an important issue, but the same position would stand if one set it forth in terms of Buddhist and Jain doctrines. Let us suppose someone reasonably well-informed about such movements as these and those of the Ajivakas and of the Buddhist *saṁgha,* the subsequent development of Buddhist separatism, the later intermingling of Buddhist and Shaiva motifs..., the final dissolving of 'Buddhism' without 'Hinduism' in India, and the emergence of 'Buddhism' outside India. I doubt that any such person could seriously maintain that the history of the fifteen hundred years preceding the Muslim invasion of India can best be conceptualised in terms of three separate religious entities labelled Hinduism, Buddhism and Jainism.[4]

It is thus my submission that in the light of the analysis of the diverse aspects of the problem of delineating the various strands of thought which constituted early Indian tradition, it will pay rich dividends to take a look at the general Indian philosophical outlook to get at the Jaina conception of philosophy.

However, before referring to the backdrop of the Indian tradition against which the Jaina concept of philosophy can be discerned, it is important to bear in mind that the term *philosophy* itself is understood in the west in different senses.[5] The divergent usages of the term and the various postulations in regard to the aim of philosophy and the implicit suggestions concerning the methodology to be adopted might all be quite helpful in appreciating the fact that within the Indian tradition itself the term philosophy can well be expected to incorporate different meanings which however are inter-related.

The obvious reason for the brief reference to the varied meanings of philosophy in the western tradition is that *philosophy* is a western term. As derived from the Greek root-words, *philos* and *sophia*, the activity called philosophising is ultimately rooted in the 'love of wisdom'. Man's curiosity to know and understand Reality perhaps resulted in his probing into its various aspects, analysing them, interpreting the aspects analysed and coming out with theories and systems. The Greek *philosophia*, as love of wisdom, generated the twin-habits of 'searching inquiry' and a ceaseless effort at 'comprehending Reality'. The rigourous exercise of the mental powers and the recognition of the need to develop the capacity for reflection and analysis have always characterised philosophy in the West; nay, they have become the dominant strains of the western philosophic enterprise in the West. The result, as the history of western philosophy shows clearly, is that divergent definitions of philosophy came to be put forward and different schools of philosophy emerged while proposing various pers-pectives and led even to a radical revision of traditionally accepted concepts of philosophy.[6]

These ideas concerning the concept of philosophy in the west, have far-reaching implications for a concept of philosophy in the Indian tradition and for the Jaina viewpoint, as an integral aspect of the Indian tradition as we propose to argue in the following pages. Since *darśana* is the nearest equivalent for *philosophy* in the Indian tradition, delineating the concept of *darśana* is quite useful here. Our argument in brief is that the various strands of meaning of the term *darśana* facilitate an appreciation of the Jaina concept of philosophy itself. The Jaina conception of philosophy may indeed be considered an articulation of aspects of the general Indian conception as discernible in the concept of *darśana*.

Darśana: The Key-word For Philosophy In The Indian Tradition

The term *darśana* is a derivative of the Sanskrit root-word *dṛś* which literally means 'to see'. What does this derivation signify for a *concept* of philosophy? 'Seeing' in the sense of receiving visual sensations by man perhaps starts the whole enterprise which goes by the name of philosophy today. Since receiving sensations (here, visual sensations) by itself is followed by the mind working on them and converting them into perception, it is highly suggestive of the fact that perceptions in general, provide significant starting points for philosophy. Hence it is not just one type of sensation, viz. visual sensation, nor one type of perception, visual perception, but the various types of sensations such as auditory, olfactory, gustatory and tactual and the various types of perception resulting consequently, that can all be referred to as *darśana*. The role played by the various sense-organs in introducing man to the world around him may thus be considered to be emphasised here.[7]

Even when this foundational idea of *darśana* is considered, it is evident how elastic the term itself is. This is also a pointer to the comprehensiveness of the term. It does not refer to perception alone but includes within its scope, conceptual knowledge as well as intuitional experience, as S. Radhakrishnan puts it.[8]

In such a conception of *darśana* as philosophy is to be found the Indian approach which, while it makes room for perception as well as inference (with the in-built provision for logic) also provides for intuitional experience. It is however important to note, even at the outset, that though *darśana* is the most popularly accepted 'equivalent' to philosophy in India, there were other terms which had been made use of earlier.[9] All the same, since the term *darśana* is most comprehensive in its import, we may confine our attention to it alone here, and comment specially on the way in which the Jaina philosophers may be visualised to have derived a new world of meaning from it.

Darśana As System of Philosophy[10]

Since the three different ingredients of philosophy referred to in the last section are found, on analysis, in the various Indian schools of philosophy, it would be apposite to indicate that *darśana* stands foremost for the idea of a 'system of philosophy'.

It is significant in this context to note that Haribhadra, a Jaina author of the 5th-6th century, gave the title *Ṣaḍdarśana-samuccaya* (A Compendium of Six Philosophies) to his work and set a precedent to the idea of referring to systems of philosophy as *darśana.* Though only six systems of philosophy are summarised in this work, the title was a forerunner of the tradition of denoting a system of philosophy by the term *darśana.* Eight centuries later, a renowned Vedāntin, Madhava summarised fifteen schools of philosophy in a work, *Sarvadarśanasaṁgraha*[11] ("A Summary of All Philosophic Systems"), making the term *darśana* even more popular as referring to a 'school of philosophy'.

The term *darśana* as standing for the various aspects of philosophical analysis was used, however, even prior to the 5th-6th centuries. The earlier usage of the term as standing for true philosophic knowledge, is found in the *Vaiśeṣika-Sūtra* of Kaṇāda which belonged perhaps to the pre-Buddhistic period. The Buddhist piṭakas (400 B.C.) called the heretical opinions *ditthi (dṛṣṭi* in Sanskrit from the same root *dṛś* from which *darśana* is formed).[12] But, judging from the fact that the very title of a work in which philosophic schools[13] were reviewed was used for the first time by a Jaina thinker, it may be surmised that it definitively fixed the meaning of *darśana* as a system of philosophic thought.

As various systems of philosophy put forth their points of view, as they represent different perspectives, it is futile to state categorically that one view *as against* all the others is the right one. This idea implicit in the idea of *darśana*[14] is explicated by the Jaina philosophers as will emerge in the sequel.

Darśana As Incorporating An In-built Logic

From the well-known fact that schools of philosophy in India, both orthodox (*āstika-darśanas*) and heterodox (*nāstika-darśanas*) have had a succession of proponents and defendants, it is easy to surmise that they all have had to rely on the process of methodically presenting their views and cogently arguing out their positions. Since the various schools of philosophy grew side by side in ancient India, extreme rigour was required in the arguments formulated by them against critics. This necessarily meant that a self-critical attitude, while founding schools and giving currency to a thesis, was required of philosophers as well as their disciples who were keen to continue the line of argument.

It might thus be suggested that the 'schools' recognized quite early in their histories, the need for a logical base for erecting the superstructure. If every school of philosophy represented a point of view that was taken, this process of taking a stand required that the thinkers had to *think out* their positions and not simply stick to a viewpoint.

Today the need for a built-in logic in any system of philosophy is accepted as vitally important but considering the fact that this requirement of a logical structure was insisted upon twenty centuries ago by Indian schools of philosophy, the importance accorded to logic as an aspect of philosophy can well be appreciated. Explaining this aspect of philosophy in classical India, a recent renowned Indian thinker writes:

> It is a Logic which is at the same time a full theory of knowledge. The problems it tackles are: (i) what is knowledge, (ii) what is its relation to object, (iii) types and sub-types of knowledge - perception, inference, etc. with sub-divisions of each, (iv) sources of valid knowledge (*pramāṇā*) in each such case, (v) the relation of knowledge to language, (vi) semantics and syntax, (vii) why and how far testimony is valid, (viii) elaborate theories of error, (ix) belief and (established) truth -what makes an awareness true, i.e. theories of validity (*prāmāṇ*ya), (x) indeterminate perception, judgmental perception and judgment, (xi) nature and types of fallacy, (xii) whether and how far memory is a source of valid knowledge, etc.[15]

It is obvious from the above that a thorough-going analysis of the logical dimension of philosophy involved going beyond the procedure of inference and examining the limitations of human reason. Reason can thus be seen to have been employed in understanding the limitations of reason. This meant for all schools of philosophy that the realm of reason had to be transcended. The scope and limits of reason thus underlined signifies that while logical analysis is an important dimension of 'doing' philosophy, it does not constitute the be-all and end-all of the discipline.[16] These ideas are clearly reflected in and elaborated by the Jaina thinkers and this will be indicated at the appropriate place.

Darśana As Intuition

The limitations of reason, as schools of Indian philosophy saw it, signified not that reason was unimportant but that beyond the region of reasoning and thought, there is an experiential realm which makes for the completion of the task of philosophy itself. While the inquiring and reflective nature of philosophy is given the importance it deserves, it is held by all the traditions of Indian philosophy that the culmination of the interrogative mode is to be found in the *transforming influence* it has on human life.

Philosophy, according to this line of thinking, is not a logical game *merely*. Though quenching the thirst of intellectual curiosity is achieved through philosophy, that is not the ultimate end envisaged. It is a means and, unless its findings are interiorised and made to become part and parcel of one's being, the philosophic pursuit itself is to be deemed incomplete and hence futile.

The close-knit relationship between rational inquiry and the experience that ought to result from it (if thought does not remain mere thought but lights up and transforms human life) as Indian thought would point out, is responsible for philosophy being considered to have a practical goal. Rather than being a mere world-view, philosophy offers a view of life which results in a way of life being adopted. Thus it is that an inquiry into the nature of Reality, - outer and inner - is considered a means to achieving an ultimate end, *spiritual freedom*. And this is variously referred to as *mokṣa, mukti, nirvāṇa, etc.*

The ultimate ideal referred to here is not considered a mental construct merely but as comprehensible only when it is realised in one's own experience. While visualising what that experience might be is worthwhile, neither verbally describing it nor rationally analysing its structure, is totally helpful. For, the realm of speculation and the thought-world of logic are characterised utmost with *mediate knowledge* and *high probability* whereas the realm of intuitive experience is characterised both by *immediacy* and *certainty*. As S. Radhakrishnan remarks, the ultimate experience "is sovereign in its own right and carries its own credentials. It is self-established (*svatassiddha*), self-evidencing (*svasaṁvedya*) and self-luminous (*svayaṁprakāśa*)."[17]

The nature of Reality revealed in intuition is held to be total and complete. Intellection alone cannot be relied upon here. For, *analysis* which is the function of the intellect, is a *necessary condition*, it is *not a sufficient condition* for getting an insight into the Totality. While perception and intellection are capable of pointing the way to Reality, it is intuition[18] which is said to help the individual 'reach' it.

Notes and References

1 See for instance, the definition of Brahmanism as "the most ancient and orthodox core of traditional Hinduism as expressed in the religious scriptures known as the Veda and related materials." - Article on "Brahmanism" in *The Encyclopaedia Americana*, Vol. IV

2 See his introduction to the section on Hinduism in Wm Theodore de Bury, edt., *Sources of Indian Tradition*, New York: Columbia University Press, 1958, pp. 3-4

3 See for instance, the detailed discussion of the term 'Hindu' in Wilfred Cantwell Smith, *The Meaning and End of Religion*, New York: The New American Library of World Literature, 1964, 61, 62 and 249.

4 *Ibid.*, pp. 250-251.

5 See the Article on *"Philosophy" Encyclopaedia of Philosophy*, Vol. V

6 The field of philosophy has not been an exception in the matter of redefining the scope and subject-matter of the discipline. The situation is neither uprising nor inexplicable. For one thing, piercing rational inquiry has been the hallmark of philosophy from its early beginnings, and for another, turning the searchlight of rational analysis on its own methods, was but a natural sequel of its reflective characteristic. The anti-metaphysical stance taken by some thinkers in the West, the great following this movement has had and the resulting definition of *philosophy as analysis*, it may be noted, has left its strong imprint on the concept of philosophy itself today.

7 This is at least one of the basic concerns in philosophy and, epistemology as an important subdivision of philosophy even in the West, would vouchsafe for the philosophic significance of the process of knowing. It is interesting to note that the very division of philosophers into *empiricists* and *rationalists* points to the foundational significance of epistemology. Man's attempting to understand the universe around him is thus considered to set the ball of philosophic inquiry rolling. The significance of *darśana* as connoting philosophy in the Indian tradition is thus obvious and hardly needs reiteration.

8 S. Radhakrishnan, *Indian Philosophy*, London: George Allen & Unwin Ltd., Vol. I, p. 43.

9 See K. Satchidananda Murty, *Philosophy in India*, Delhi: Motilal Banarsidass, 1985, pp. 3-7 for a more detailed consideration of these.

10 *Ṣaḍdarśanasamuccaya*. (See English trans. by K. Satchidananda Murty, Tenali : Tagore Publishing House, 1957)

11 *Sarvadarśanasaṁgraha*, (See English trans. by E.B. Cowell & A.E. Gough edited by K.L.Joshi, Delhi : Parimal Publications, 1981)

12 S.N. Dasgupta, A *History of Indian Philosophy*, Cambridge: Cambridge University Press, 1922, Vol. I, p. 68 (f.n.)

13 The six systems of philosophy referred to by Haribhadra, however, are : Nyāya, Vaiśeṣika, Sāṅkhya, Mimāṁsā, Jainism and Buddhism. since Nyāya and Vaiśeṣika are identified with each other, Cārvāka materialism is counted as the sixth. We find this system too treated in Haribhadra's work. The present practice, however is to refer to the orthodox Hindu systems of thought (Nyāya, Vaiśeṣika, Sāṅkhya, Yoga, Mīmāṁsa and Vedānta) alone as the 'six systems'. The other three, referred to as *nāstika-darśanas*, are Jainism, Buddhism and Cārvāka.

14 See *supra*, p.6, para 4

15 Kalidas Bhattacharya, "Traditional Indian Philosophy As a Modern Indian Thinker Views It" in S.S. Rama Rao Pappu and R. Puligandla, edt., *Indian Philosophy: Past and Future*, Delhi: Motilal Banarsidass, 1982, p.183.

16 See *supra*, p.6, para 3

17 *An Idealist View of Life*, London: George Allen & Unwin Ltd., 1932, p. 92

18 See *supra*, p. 6, para 3

Chapter Two
JAINISM AS METAPHILOSOPHY

In the light of the three meanings of the term *darśana* as used in the Indian tradition as the nearest equivalent of *philosophy* and, in terms of the suggestion that these 'meanings' of philosophy find an articulation in the Jaina tradition, we may enquire further as to how to arrive at the Jaina concept of philosophy.

It seems to me that the ideas of *content* and *method* provide useful starting points in our enquiry. It is obvious, even at the outset, that the two are related so closely that the consideration of the one cannot be attempted without an analysis of the other. The term 'content' may be understood, in general terms, as referring to the subject-matter; and, by 'method' is meant the techniques adopted by different systems (of philosophy) to deal with the subject-matter.

Concerned as we are with an enquiry into the concept of philosophy as discernible in the Jaina tradition, suffice it to state here that the theme subjected to analysis is the nature of Reality.[1] As man cannot be considered apart from Reality, reflection about the human condition is considered an equally legitimate subject-matter of philosophy.

Arriving at the Jaina concept of philosophy may thus be attempted by delineating some details of its *Weltanschauung*. But here again what needs to be remembered is that these details *qua* details are not important for our specific task.These are to be considered with a view to identifying areas of enquiry which are crucial for philosophical analysis itself.

The Jaina philosophers throughout point to the fact that Reality is an extremely comprehensive term. For, it not merely incorporates a view of the nature of the universe but also a general philosophy of life. But for the presence of the latter element, the Jaina theory would have remained a mere intellectual construction of a world-view, - describing natural phenomena and analysing the laws which are at work.

While reference to matter constitutes the hard-core analysis of one aspect of Reality, the physical universe, reference to consciousness points to the other aspect, the non-physical. The implicit suggestion here is that leaving either of the aspects out of account is tantamount to taking a one-sided view of Reality, and hence arriving at an incomplete picture of Reality.

The uncompromising stand of realism that Jainism takes is evident from its identification of Reality with Existence. The emphatic realistic stance of the tradition is further evident from its maintaining that Existence is Real. The assertion that the individual soul, matter, space, time and the principles of motion and rest found in the universe are all *real*[2] is indeed a clear indication that both the conscious and the non-conscious aspects of Reality (*jīva and ajīva*) do exist. The six ultimate categories listed above and referred to as the two aspects of Reality are also denoted by the term *dravya* (Substance).

Since all the six categories are existent and are capable of assuming different modes and exhibiting varying qualities, Jainism defines *dravya* as follows: "That which maintains its identity while manifesting its various qualities and modifications and which is not different from *Sattā* (existence) is called *dravya*."[3]

The three aspects of Substance just mentioned need to be reflected about to get at the Jaina theory of Reality. The term *sat* (existence) signifies the substantiality of the world outside the perceiver's mind. The world of matter and non-matter is not a mere construction of the mind. It has its independent existence in *rerum natura*. This is perhaps what is meant by the statement: "Essentially, substance does not change."[4]

The 'qualities' and 'modifications' refer to the appearance-aspect of Reality. They point to the eternality-aspect of Substance in so far as Substance is regarded neither as created nor as destroyed. The essential nature of clay remaining unchanged despite its possible modes (shapes it assumes) and the varying qualities (colour, etc) it exhibits, is cited as an illustration.

The Jaina philosophers maintain that the persistent or enduring aspect of Substance is quite evident from the very attempt at understanding the changes that take place in a thing since the attempt presupposes that the thing itself persists in spite of the changes. The changing modes are referred to variously as appearance and disappearance, origination and decay, modification, becoming, difference, discreetness, plurality, manyness and manifoldness. This seems to be the point made by Umāswāmi in his cryptic statement that *sat* possess origination (*utpāda*), decay (*vyaya*) and permanence *dhruvatva*."[5]

Furthermore, describing the diverse qualities or ascribing attributes of different kinds implies that something exists; it is of this something that the various qualities are postulated. Speaking meaningfully of qualities, the Jaina philosopher asserts, is synonymous with asserting the existence of a substratum, an entity which is at its base. Similarly pointing to the changing modes too signifies, nay presupposes the assertion of a substance, for the changes in the modes must relate to something which persists[6] through all the changes.

It is significant here to note that the Jaina philosophers' assertion that the conscious as well as non-conscious aspects of Reality exist as also their unambiguous position that Reality as Substance exists in three states, viz. permanence (*dhruvatva*), appearance (*utpāda*) and disappearance (*vyaya*) imply that the three states relate to the *jīva*-aspect as well as the *ajīva*-aspect. The point is especially made here to indicate the direction that the analysis of *jīva* (along these lines) takes.

The changing modes of the *jīva* point to the four states of being (*gati*), viz. those of infernal beings (*nāraki*), animals (*tiryañc*), human beings (*manuṣya*) and celestial beings (*devatā*). The varying qualities of consciousness indicate the relation into which the *jīva* enters when it comes into contact with the *ajīva*-aspect of Reality. In every one of these stages the *jīva* undergoes real changes, though its identity itself is not lost. The changes are seen in the facts of birth, growth and death.

Due to its association with *karma*[7] (an aspect of *ajīva*) the *jīva* gets bound and is caught up in the cycle of birth and death. Association with *karma* is considered a mark of impurity and hence the *jīva* in the state of bondage is referred to as impure (*aśuddha*). With the attainment of liberation (*mokṣa*), the *jīva* becomes pure (*śuddha*). The original state of purity of consciousness which was lost (thanks to the impact of *ajīva*, - particularly karmic matter, an aspect of *ajīva*) is now regained.

From our brief reference above to the Jaina *Weltanschauung* the general drift of Jaina philosophy would have become apparent: the analysis of Reality includes a concept of man as well as an exhortation that a right understanding of Reality paves the way for realising a practical end for which philosophy strives.[8]

Our analysis of the Jaina viewpoint has thusfar been deliberately directed on the *content-aspect* rather than on the methodological aspect. Why has this procedure been adopted even though our main concern is arriving at a concept of philosophy? Our answer is that it is with a view to making the point that descriptions of various systems of philosophy focus on content rather than on the method of analysis involved. It is also with a view to underlining the fact that not only are there systems of philosophy (*darśanas*) but patterns of analysis as well which are at work in them all.

The patterns may not be discernible at all unless they are deliberately pondered over. This indeed makes it difficult to arrive at a concept of philosophy. Why are the patterns not transparently evident at first sight and why cannot a concept of philosophy make itself apparent, even to start with? While describing the systems (delineating the specific contents of the system in question) is comparatively an easy task, "going beyond the contents", reflecting about what is involved in constructing these systems of philosophy, is admittedly a more difficult task. How is this situation to be accounted for? A slight digression here in defining the term *metaphilosophy* itself might help in finding the answer to our query.

While the expression 'philosophising' might be rightly used to describe what the various systems attempt to explain, the term 'philosophising about philosophy' may be employed to go beneath the superstructure that these systems of philosophy represent. This is the idea of metaphilosophy as employed in our present enquiry into the Jaina concept of philosophy. The question posed in the previous paragraph might then be rephrased as follows: "Why is a philosophy of philosophy (metaphilosophy) more difficult to arrive at than understanding philosophy as denoting systems of philosophy?"

A recent renowned Indian philosopher offers this answer to our queries. "Instances of philosophy occur first", he observes, and continues: "and this enables us to raise a general question regarding its nature."[9] He adds : "...the elucidation of the concept of philosophy is more difficult than the exposition of a philosophical system. For, the former is a question of the second order, of a deeper layer underlying the overt and avowed one... philosophy of philosophy... stands on a deeper level of reflective consciousness."[10]

In our terms: investigating the question as to what is involved in arriving at philosophical positions or building systems of philosophy is more difficult than 'describing' a philosophical system. Since the latter is thus admittedly an easier task, it is natural to look into it first. And because it is closely related to the more difficult question of the methodology at work (in building the system of philosophy), the concrete doctrines and theories themselves are quite helpful in identifying the presuppositions of the philosophical system itself.

This has been the *rationale* behind our outlining the Jaina view (philosophy of Jainism) for delineating the concept of philosophy implicit in it. Before proceeding further it may well be tc spell it out. In this context three lines of analysis in regard to philosophy can be visualised:

1. What is the scope and subject-matter of philosophy?
2. If philosophy is understood as a *system*, what are the methods employed in this process of system-building?
3. What is the purpose of philosophising?

In regard to the first question, the Jaina view, as has been indicated by considering its view of Substance, is that Reality is the subject-matter of philosophy. The scope of philosophical analysis, however is not to be restricted to considering any one aspect of Reality, however important it might be.

For the sake of convenience, two aspects of the analysis may be more specifically commented upon, viz. the objective and the subjective. The former which has also been quite often referred to as the *outer* or *external* aspects, may be conceded as striking the attention of the philosopher at first. It is because of this that the nature of the world 'outside', the phenomena observable through perception and the characteristics they possess are at first looked into. While attempting to understand external Reality, however a deeper probe into the relationship between the observed phenomena and the features they possess, results. This technically is the *problem of Substance and attributes*. In addition, observance of a sequential relationship between phenomena leads to analysis of the precise relationship between them. This broadly indicates the philosophers' concern with the universal law of causation. The systematic characteristic of the universe and the existence of a meaningful structure seem to suggest themselves as a result.

Sooner or later, attention of the philosopher is inevitably turned on the inner world of human experience; and, questions hitherto posed in regard to the outer world are now addressed to the internal aspects of *one's existence* and transformed into a deeper analysis of the subjective aspects of existence in general. What is important to note here is that there is not only an attempt at finding, within the internal world of human experience, correlates of principles at work in the external world but also an effort at comprehending the differentiating characteristics of the inner world itself. While 'substantiality' and 'existence' may be considered "shared characteristics" possessed by the outer and the inner aspects of Reality respectively, the distinguishing feature of the latter is identified as the possession of consciousness.

The Jaina theory of *ajīva* and *jīva* referred to briefly in an earlier section may thus be seen to imply a concerted attempt at comprehending the nature of Reality from the objective and the subjective angles respectively. It implies further that analysis of Reality cannot be confined to the outer aspects alone though the process (of analysis) may commence with the 'external'. Thirdly, since the analysis of Reality is attempted by man who is in quest of understanding it, the identification of the subjective aspects inevitably signifies for man also a right understanding of himself as an aspect of Reality and more especially the way he is related to it.

This indeed makes for an understanding of Reality which is not directed merely at an examination of the *status quo* but a reflection of what ought to be the case. The dissatisfaction with the *status quo* may be considered to give impetus to this search for the understanding of the *right relationship* between man's innermost being and the peripheral aspects of his own personality on the one hand and, on the other, to the comprehension of the non-conscious aspects of Reality. This may be a starting point of philosophic enquiry itself which has to culminate in achieving a state of being which would bring with it a wholesome feeling of having found the true nature of oneself.

In this sense, reflecting about Reality does not connote a cold, analytical consideration of it but a more involved approach. As this involvement is of man's whole being and not merely his intellectual aspect, the comprehension of Reality resulting from it can be expected to bring with it a whole new outlook on life and things and also a transformed personality.

Considered in this light, the complexity of the Real - whether looked at from the outside or from the inside - is all too evident. Also, since both the outer (understood as the 'universe around') and the inner (interpreted as the 'human universe' proper) aspects of Reality are themselves subjected to further analyses and yield a varied and manifold picture, dogmatising on the validity or correctness of any one view of Reality or any specific approach to Reality (as against all others) would seem to need a critical evaluation.

The subject-matter of philosophy being thus considered to be the *whole of Reality,* - neither the objective aspects alone nor the subjective aspects merely, but both together considered as aspects of a totality - the scope of philosophy is indeed very vast. Every attempt to understand Reality would be valuable and they may all be looked upon as offering creative possibilities of comprehension. Read along with the idea that understanding Reality is not merely a cognitive effort at mental comprehension but a whole new attempt at getting to 'know' it in *all* its aspects, the rich scope offered by the varied attempts at philorophising is abundantly clear. Consequently, the methods adopted in the process of philosophising can also be expected to be various and effective in revealing the variegated nature of Reality.

Methods of Philosophy

The consideration of the subject-matter and scope of philosophy in the previous section has indicated that the complex nature of Reality and the vast scope for philosophic discussion it offers are highly suggestive of various methods that need to be employed in the process.

If, in philosophy, knowledge of the whole of Reality is what counts ultimately (in so far as Reality *is* the subject-matter of philosophy), the question as to *how* this knowledge is to be obtained, suggests itself as the logically next one. In this sense, the expression "the methods of philosophy" should be understood more concretely as "methods by employing which knowledge of Reality can be acquired."

Since knowledge presupposes the knower as well as the object(s) he wants to know (also referred to as objects of knowledge), enquiring into the *means* by which the former acquires a knowledge of the latter comes to be regarded as vitally important while analysing how the knower can know the object. The means of knowing are referred to as *pramāṇa*.

It is contextually important to recount here that while the ancient Hindu philosophers considered in detail both the means of knowing (*pramāṇa*) and the objects of knowledge (*prameya*), the Jaina philosophers confined their attention to the idea of *pramāṇa* alone. The implication of this emphasis on the 'means of knowing' is perhaps that focusing on the ways of getting knowledge is more specifically called for while discussing the methods of philosophy. A well-known scholar of Indian logic explains the situation as follows:

> The ancient logic dealt with sixteen categories such as pramāṇa, prameya, etc. comprising such heterogeneous elements as doctrine of salvation and nature of the soul, etc. The medieval logic (which includes the Jaina and the Buddhist views*), on the contrary, concerns itself with one category, viz. *pramāṇa*, which touches upon other categories only in so far as these are necessary for its proper elaboration.[11]

Primacy is given to the *pramāṇa*-aspect of the knowing process since a consideration of it would *per force* include an analysis of the objects regarding which knowledge is sought. Hence an elaborate reflection on the *pramāṇas* would vouchsafe for a synoptic view of the knowledge-situation.

What is even more significant is that in Jainism "the doctrine of *pramāṇa* is treated in such a way that it may be equally applied to the ...systems of the Brahmaṇas (Hindus*), Jainas and Buddhists."[12] This is perhaps one other reason why the Jaina concept of philosophy can be hoped to be explicated by considering the way they dealt with philosophical problems.

Furthermore, in the Jaina tradition inference (*anumāna*), one of the kinds of *pramāṇa*, received an elaborate treatment. A full-fledged theory of syllogism was also proposed.[13] This would signify that the Jaina philosophers highlighted the important role played by logic in the process of philosophising, - in the process of building systems of philosophy as we have preferred to refer to it.

However, it should not be mistaken that the Jaina philosophers considered logic as the 'ultimate method' in philosophy. For, the doctrine of *pramāṇa* held by them points to a stage where even the logical methods employed are to be set aside as ultimately not crucial.

The idea can be made clear by briefly referring to the various *pramāṇas* accepted by the Jaina philosophers. One of the renowned Jaina philosophers, Umāsvāti writes : " Knowledge is of five varieties, viz. *mati, śruta, avadhi, manaḥparyāya* and *kevala*. All these varieties are *pramāṇa*." [14]

Of these five means, *mati-jñāna* stands for determinate knowledge derived through the sense-organs and the mind. *Śruta-jñāna* stands for scriptural or verbal knowledge. This kind of knowledge also stands for knowledge derived through words which are symbols of thought, gestures, etc. *Avadhi-jñāna* is determinate knowledge of physical objects derived directly by the knower without the instrumentality of either the sense-organs or the mind. *Manaḥparyāya-jñāna* refers to the knowledge of other minds, i.e. the thoughts of the others. *Kevala-jñāna* is the determinate and unlimited knowledge of the whole of Reality that the individual derives directly.[15] Of the five types of knowledge *mati* and *śruta* are referred to as mediate or indirect (*parokṣa*)[16] and *avadhi, manaḥparyāya* and *kevala* are referred to as immediate or direct (*pratyakṣa*).[17]

It would have become evident from the above classification of the *pramāṇas* that the importance accorded to *pramāṇa* well indicates the roles played by the sense-organs (as evidenced by the acceptance of perception as a source of knowledge) as well as the mind (as is obvious from the Jaina philosophers' conceding the inferential-logical processes as providing another means of knowing). All the same, envisaging knowledge (of Reality) as attainable without the help of either the sense-organs or the mind (as is indicated by the three other *pramāṇas*) would point to the Jaina view that the perceptual mode as well as the logical mood will have to be transcended. As a knowledge of the whole of Reality is said to be attainable only by such a transcendence of the perceptual and inferential methods, it is suggested that ordinary methods of knowledge are not efficacious to 'know' Reality.

What is the purpose of philosophising?

The acceptance of the limitations of the knowing process when it solely relies upon the sense-organs and the mind would suggest indirectly that the purpose of philosophising cannot be confined to the empirical processes of perception and analysing the knowledge so received. Notwithstanding the worthwhileness of the logical procedures which enable one to go beyond what is actually given to the sense-organs, it cannot be gainsaid that the very complex nature of Reality imposes limitations even on the reasoning faculty.

It would also suggest that "gaining knowledge of Reality" (the aim of philosophy) would not be possible only through *intellectual comprehension* of the complex texture of Reality in so far as intellection refers verily to the functioning of the sense-organs and the mind. Whether through gaining a perceptual base or through erecting a superstructure with the help of logic, the cognitive mode of gaining a knowledge of Reality is seen indeed to be limited in scope. And this perhaps impels man to go beyond the limitations imposed and transcend the empirical realms of the knowing process itself.

Once again the reasoning process comes in handy. For, with its help a transcendental state of knowing is visualised. Since the passage of thought generally is from the known to the unknown, and since what is known is recognised to be 'limited', what is yet to be known is inferred as 'unlimited'. 'The transcendental state of knowing' mentioned just now refers to the ascent of knowledge to the hitherto unknown regions. Also, since the limited knowledge gained thusfar is recognised as being due to the working of the sense-organs and the mind, it occurs to the questing mind that the limitations can be hoped to be overcome only by 'going beyond'. The idea derived is that the sense-organs and the mind are positive obstructions in the path of gaining complete understanding,- in reaching out to a fuller knowledge of Reality.

Furthermore, the varying degrees of knowledge gained would suggest a summit, - a peak - which represents the culmination of the entire process of knowing This may be referred to as the state of full knowledge, all-knowingness or omniscience. Every step ascended would indicate not merely a greater degree of knowledge, both quantitatively and qualitatively, but also progressive success registered in the matter of overcoming the obstructions in order to gain omniscience.[18]

This then is the goal of philosophy according to the Jaina philosophers. *Kevala-jñāna* is the term used and it is referred to variously as *direct knowledge, immediate perception,* etc.[19] It is defined as perfect (*paripūrṇa*), complete (*samagra*), unique (*asādhāraṇa*), absolute (*nirapekṣa*), pure (*viśuddha*), all-comprehensive (*sarva-bhāva-jñāpaka*), that which has for its object both the world and the non-world (*lokalokaviṣaya*) and infinite (*anantaparyāya*).[20]

The definition implies that the omniscient stage in the human pursuit of knowledge is the stage where Reality is intuited fully without any obstruction whatsoever. The further implication of the definition is that the omniscient stage represents also the transcendence of the spatial and temporal categories. Omniscience is hence regarded as one wholesome experience which does not incorporate within itself limitations characteristic of experience in space and time.

The superiority of *kevala-jñāna* is asserted on the ground that the objects of *mati* and *śruta* are *all* the substances, but not in all their aspects (*asarva-dravyeṣu asarva-paryāyeṣu*), of *avadhi*, only material substances, but not in all their aspects (*rūpiṣveva dravyeṣu asarva paryāyeṣu*); *manaḥparyāya* is a purer and infinitely subtle knowledge of the material substances known by *avadhi*; and *kevala* has for its object all the substances, and in all their aspects (*sarvadravyeṣu sarva- paryāyeṣu ca*).[21]

The consummation of all knowledge in *kevala-jñāna* is also pointed to by referring to a Jaina tradition which holds that when *kevala-jñāna* is attained, the other four types of knowledge, viz. *mati, śruta, avadhi* and *manaḥparyāya* disappear much in the same way as the other luminous objects in the sky lose their luminosity when the sun appears on the firmament. The argument offered in this regard is that *kevala-jñāna* is due to the total destruction of the *jñānāvaraṇa-karma* whereas the other four are due only to the destruction-cum-subsidence of the *jñānāvaraṇa-karma*.[22] Total destruction (of the obstructive factors) has the possibility of destruction-cum-subsidence.[23]

Such a concept of *kevala-jñāna* is understandable also from the Jaina view that the human soul has the *potentiality* to know *all things in all their aspects*, i.e. to know the whole of Reality. The Jaina philosophers have prescribed a course of ethical discipline for actualising the potentiality. For our present discussion, the details (of the ethical prescriptions) as such are not important.[24]

What is significant, however is the Jaina philosophers' pointing out that the human potential indicates that obstructions to knowledge are not complete. For, there would then be no distinction between the soul (*jīva*) and the non-soul (*ajīva*). This means further that the absence of total obstruction to knowledge signifies that the limited capacity to know is seen in the sense-organs and the mind enabling us to get *some knowledge* of Reality; as such, the validity of knowledge so acquired cannot be disputed.

This has an important implication for arriving at the Jaina concept of philosophy and it may be briefly indicated here. The idea that the limited knowledge gained of Reality through empirical methods of knowing is valuable as far as it goes, is itself suggestive of the need for attaining a transcendental viewpoint (*dravyārthika-naya* in contradistinction to the empirical view point (*paryāyārthika-naya*). By proposing such a distinction between the two points of view, Jainism seems to indicate how various metaphysical systems (systems of philosophy) should be understood in relation to one another and how these should be accepted as valuable contributions to an understanding of Reality without, however tacitly acquiescing in their claims to absolute validity.

Thus it is that Jainism emerges as metaphilosophy; for here is a critical approach adopted to the very process of system-building. This idea of philosophy of philosophy arrived at through the critical method is explicated in two of the celebrated theories put forward by the Jaina philosophers, and to a consideration of them, we shall now turn.

Notes and References

1 This is not to suggest that in the other schools of Indian philosophy, - orthodox and heterodox - discussion of the nature of Reality is not the main concern. It should be positively conceded that the dominant characteristic of Indian systems of philosophy in general (the *cārvāka* materialist's position being an exception) is their building systems of thought on the strong foundations of metaphysics. Even though the point may be contested by some scholars from the point of view of early Buddhism, it should be remembered that despite the fact that the Buddha was averse to dwelling on metaphysical issues, a metaphysical view is discernible in his thought. In fact the metaphysical system-building found in the various schools may even be regarded as occasioning the implicit and explicit criticism of the way systems of philosophy have proceeded. And, Jainism as *metaphilosophy* is identifiable precisely in the philosophers of this tradition suggesting how systems of philosophy should and should not be built.

2 See *Bhagavatī-Sūtra*, xxv, 2-4.

3 *Pañcāstikāya*, 8.

4 *Sarvārthasiddhi*, V. 30.

5 *Tattvārtha-Sūtra*, V. 29.

6 Being, identity, non-difference (and) continuance are also terms which are used as equivalents of the term permanence (*dhruvatva*), observes a scholar. - See Y. J. Padmarajiah, *Jaina Theories of Reality and Knowledge*, Bombay: Jain Sahitya Vikas Mandal, 1963, p. 127.

7 One of the distinguishing features of Jainism is that it regards *karma* as an aggregate of extremely fine matter which is imperceptible to the senses. The binding effect of *karma* is explained in terms of the various stages through which kārmic particles are attracted towards the *jīva*, thanks to the attitudes of attachment and aversion developed, and engulf it finally. As matter (*pudgala*) is an aspect of the category of *ajīva* (the non-conscious principle), the contact of *jīva* with *ajīva* is regarded as instrumental to the state of bondage.

8. This signifies that the Jaina system of ethics is grounded on its metaphysics. The analysis of Reality has implications for the

Jaina theory of ethics. As such, comprehending the nature of Reality is not of theoretical interest merely. Understanding Reality is to have a transformational influence on the attitude of man, and this is indicative of the practical nature of philosophy itself.

9 T.R.V. Murti, "The Concept of philosophy" in Harold Coward, edt. *Studies in Indian Thought*, Delhi: Motilal Banarsidass, 1983, p. 393.

10 *Ibid.*

11 Satis Chandra Vidyabhusana, *A History of Indian Logic*, Delhi: Motilal Banarsidass, 1978 (first published, 1970), p. 158.

12 *Ibid.*

13 See Bhadrabāhu's *Daśavaikālikaniryukti* in which is elaborated a ten-membered syllogism (*daśāvayava-vākya*). The ten members are: (i) The Proposition (*Pratijñā*), (ii) The limitation of the proposition (*pratijñā- vibhakti*), (iii) The reason (*hetu*), (iv) The limitation of reason (*hetu-vibhakti*), (v) The counter proposition (*vipakṣa*), (vi) The opposition to the counter-proposition (*vipakṣapratiṣedha*), (vii) An Example (*dṛṣṭānta*), (viii) Questioning the validity of the example (*āśanka*), (ix) The meeting of the question (*āśanka-pratiṣedha*) and (x) Conclusion (*nigamana*).

The Jainas characterise a syllogism of ten parts as the best (*uttama*), a syllogism of five parts as the mediocre (*madhyama*) and a syllogism of two parts as the worst (*jaghanga*) - See S.C. Vidyabhusana, *Op. Cit.*, p. 166 f.n.

14 *Tattvārtha-Sūtra*, I. 9-10.

cf. *Bhagavatī-Sūtra*, 88. 2. 317 which refers to the five types of knowledge as *abhinibodhika, śruta, avadhi, manaḥparyāya* and *kevala.*

N. Tatia observes that the *Agama* theory of knowledge is very old and probably originated in the pre Mahāvira period. - See *Studies in Jaina Philosophy*, Banaras: Jain Cultural Research Society, 1951, p. 27.

15 See the present author's *Outlines of Jainism*, New Delhi : Wiley Eastern Ltd., 1973, pp. 48-49.

16 *Tattvārtha-Sūtra*, I. 11.

17 *Ibid.*, I. 12.

18 See *Pramāṇa-Mimāṁsa*, I. 1. 16: "The proof of omniscience follows from the proof of the necessity of the final consummation of the progressive development of cognition." Explaining this, M.L. Mehta writes: "Just as heat is subject to varying degrees and consequently reaches the highest limit, so also cognition which is subject to progressive development owing to the varying degrees of destruction of the obscuring veil, reaches the highest limit, i.e. omniscience when the hindrance of the obscuring *karma* is totally annihilated." - See *Outlines of Jaina Philosophy*, Bangalore: Jain Mission Society, 1954, p. 100.

19 The reference is to indicate that a type of knowledge can be visualised in which the mediation of the sense-organs and the mind is significantly absent. Since there is no mediator, the *jīva* is able to have knowledge *directly*. Though clairvoyance (*avadhi-jñana*) and telepathy (*manaḥparyāya-jñāna*) also come under the category of immediate perception (*pratyakṣa*) rather than mediate perception (*parokṣa*), it is *kevala-jñāna* alone which is *immediate perception* in the full sense of the term.

20 *Tattvārtha-Sūtra*, I. 30 and Commentary.

21 *Ibid.*, I. 27-30 and Commentary.

22 *Ibid.*, I. 30 and Commentary; see also *Āvaśyakaniryukti*, 77.

23 See *Tattvārtha-Sūtra*, Commentary on I. 30.

24 See the present author's *Outlines of Jainism*, pp. 168-170 and pp. 177-179 for a more detailed analysis.

Chapter Three

PHILOSOPHY AS CRITICISM - I

Towards the close of the last chapter it emerged that Jainism as *metaphilosophy* is identifiable in its suggesting the adoption of a critical method in and through two celebrated theories. These are the theories which focus on the complex nature of Reality and the need for synthesising the various theories and respectively réferred to as *Anekāntavāda* and *Syādvāda*. In the present chapter we shall consider the first one and, in the next, the second.

As indicated earlier[1] we shall adopt the procedure of looking into the content-aspects as well as the methodological aspects of the two theories for arriving at the Jaina concept of philosophy. With this in view we shall refer to the *details* of the two theories (to the extent necessary) and also examine the *implications* of these to fulfill our main task in this study.

But, since the method in general is indicated as *critically looking at theories proposed,* we shall commence with a comment on the Jaina philosophers' insistence on evaluating 'rival claims', - their visualising the task of a philosopher who is to contend with divergent positions demanding a hearing and clamouring for consideration.

Taking positions in philosophy is noted as a 'given fact' in the sense that the existence of various schools of philosophy imply that they have taken divergent standpoints.[2] In line with our earlier comment[3] we may reiterate that one of the most crucial aspects of building up systems of philosophy is proposing a theory in regard to the nature of Reality.

Jainism as metaphilosophy suggests that the philosopher, rather than taking positions as they are *given*, i.e. without any reflection, should scrutinise them carefully. Acceptance of the truth or validity of *any system* should be done only after a careful consideration of the claims made on their behalf. This is particularly necessary since the claims made by the various schools of thought are found to have the effect of *contesting* the positions taken by the others. The claims are made with a view to asserting that they (*each one* of the rival schools) have nothing but *the whole truth* in their possession and, as such, the 'others' are totally wrong.

A careful reflection about the philosophic scene portrayed above would make clear at least one thing. Even a cursory survey of the various claims and counter-claims would indicate that the subject-matter they are all analysing is *complex.* The implicit suggestion here is that if Reality were a simple entity, understanding it would not have posed any problem and consequently there would have been no disputes in regard to describing its nature. Hence it would follow that the various theories proposed are nothing but divergent attempts at unravelling the (complex) nature of Reality.

However it should be noted that the Jaina philosophers do not argue for the complexity of Reality only on the ground that there are different approaches to Reality and correspondingly different descriptions of it. Since the implicit Jaina criticism of rival schools of thought is found in the theory that Reality is complex, this idea itself will have to be dwelt at some length before proceeding further.

Anekāntavāda as indicating the complex nature of Reality

Though the Jaina view of the complex nature of Reality has been indicated in another context in this study,[4] the idea of complexity has not been explicated in our earlier reference. In this section we shall attempt this task to get at the Jaina contention that if Reality is complex, simple, categorical statements proposed by schools of philosophy are all to be critically viewed.

The idea of complexity of Reality is discernible first in the Jaina acceptance of *many Reals*, even though they may be classified under the one or the other of the two categories, viz. the conscious Real (*jīva*) and the non-conscious Real (*ajīva*). This distinction is a fundamental one, argues a scholar and he elaborately and forcefully holds that once the *principle of distinction* is accepted, the Jaina theory of Reality as manifold (*anekānta*) cannot but be reached. Once the duality of mind and matter (or the material world) is conceded and the operative principle of distinction is allowed to run its full course, the theory of manifoldness of Reality and knowledge has to be reached as its logical terminus, he maintains. Referring to the five constituents of *Ajīva*, viz. matter (*pudgala*), space (*ākāśa*), time (*kāla*), the medium of motion (*dharma*) and the medium of rest (*adharma*), he shows that an analysis of them all reveals a pluralistic universe. He adds that Reality is not merely to be considered a complex of manyness (*aneka*) but also as manifold (*anekānta*) since each one of the multiplicity of reals is, in turn manifold or complex to its core.[5] As another author puts it, the central thesis of the Jaina is that there is not only diversity but each real is equally diversified.[6] Here it would suffice to illustrate the idea by referring to matter and space, since these are generally admitted as constituting vital aspects of an analysis of the material aspects of the universe.

In determining the ultimate constituents of matter, the method of division is considered by the Jaina philosophers to be helpful. When any object is divided, the parts obtained by division can be further divided but the process of division cannot be indefinitely continued; for, in the process a position is reached when no further division is possible. This is truly the ultimate constituent of matter, - referred to by the term *aṇu* or *paramāṇu* (atom) - in Jaina philosophy.[7] The combination of atoms gives rise to molecules referred to as *skandha* in Jainism.[8] It is the combination of molecules that is responsible for the different types of objects, possessing varying qualities.[9]

In regard to space (*ākāśa*), it is first divided into *lokākāśa* and *alokākāśa*. In the first all substances are considered to exist. It corresponds to what is generally referred to as the physical universe. In the second nothing exists. It is beyond the physical universe[10] and, as such it may be referred to as pure or 'outer' space. The physical universe is considered to be divisible and is regarded as consisting of an infinite number of space-points (*pradeśas*).[11] The manifoldness of space is thus evident.[12]

The individual soul which is an aspect of *Jīva* is considered one among the infinitely many centres of experience that can be visualised.

It may be considered to represent the subjective aspect of the manifold Reality. As has been pointed out: "This manifold nature of *jīva* is evident in every one of the infinite states (*anantabhāvas* or *pariṇāmas*) as well as in the multiple powers which are attributed to it."[13] Since the *jīva* has the power to comprehend the entire universe which is infinitely complex, its experiential powers indeed must be manifold, or commensurate with the complexity of the experienced universe. This is the implication of the statement: "the difference in the cognised (*viṣaya*) signifies a corresponding difference in the cognition (*vikalpa*) concerned."[14]

We want to argue further that the notion of manifoldness is to be understood in a deeper sense still. Though many of the traditional metaphysical problems (raised by philosophers, both in the East and in the West,—by classical as well as modern philosophers) can be analysed to indicate the deeper sense of manifoldness of Reality as understood in Jainism, we shall consider the problem of Substance alone in view of its foundational significance.

The basic issues in regard to the problem of Substance are the following: Does only the *Substance* exist and *not* the *modes*? Does the notion of *qualities* require, as a substratum, the idea of Substance? The questions can be considered as posing the problem of accepting Substance alone as existent and rejecting both modes and qualities.

The basic Jaina position is stated in a forthright manner by Umāswāmi who first defines the notion of existence and then of Substance. In regard to the first he observes: "What there is (existent) is endowed with the triple character, origin, decay and stability (persistence)."[15] From the comment that those which originate, persist, and change (disappear) are (also) possessed of the nature of Substance[16] it is clear that the changing modes as well as the qualitative changes undergone by the Substance are also real. In regard to the second, viz. the definition of Substance, the cryptic aphorism reads: "The Substance possesses qualities and modes."[17] 'Quality' is defined in a later aphorism as "that which is found in a Substance."[18] Though no definition of *mode* is given, the commentary on the *sūtra* defining *quality* throws some light on it, especially by differentiating the *mode* from *quality* by stating as follows:

> Though modes too are found in the Substance they are subject to appearance and disappearance. In this sense they are not always found in a Substance. the qualities, on the contrary, are permanent; hence are they always found in a Substance.[19]

It is also significant that another commentator addresses himself specifically to the issue of drawing a distinction between qualities and modes. He observes:

> A quality is (actually) the distinguishing character of one Substance from another. For example, the person (soul) is different from matter (non-soul) through (the possession of) cognition, etc.; matter is distinguished from soul through qualities like colour. The generic attributes common to souls are cognition, etc. and that of non-soul are colour, etc. The modifications of these qualities, viewed in their particular nature, are called modes such as: cognition of a pot, anger, pride (in a soul); and intense or mild odour, deep or light colour in the case of the non-soul.[20]

From the brief consideration of the question whether modes and qualities are real and if so, in what sense, it has emerged that since they are inseparable from the notion of Substance, they are also real, but in the sense of indicating *changes* in the *persistent* Substance. Since Substance itself has been visualised as persisting through changes, it is clear that Jainism accepts both the notions of *persistence* and *change*.

In terms of distinct metaphysical positions that have been taken by certain schools of philosophy in India,[21] the Jaina view can be stated as accepting the idea of *Being* as well as *Becoming*. The acceptance of the notion of Being is evident from the definition of Substance as existent and real. And conceding the other notion is expressed explicitly by referring to changing modes and varying qualities in a Substance.

By rejecting neither Being nor Becoming and, in the process, accepting both as necessary and important for understanding the concept of Substance, the Jaina philosophers indicate the complex nature of Reality. Though the above discussion was specifically about Substance, one aspect of Reality, it is obvious how the idea of complexity of Reality is espoused. It can be explained thus: Since Substance is a *complex* of its Being-aspect and Becoming-aspect, if the persistent-aspect is highlighted, we are dwelling on the Being-aspect of Reality and if the changing-aspect is focused upon, we are referring to the Becoming-aspect of Reality.

The description of Substance or of an object in the world (to clarify the notion of 'description') may also be understood in two different ways. One way of portrayal of the object would be to explain how it continues to exist. "The fact of the matter is", it might be emphasised, "the object of reference continues to exist despite the changes that may take place in it, be it in the modes or in the qualities." From this viewpoint it might be argued further that to get at the nature of the objects, we have to 'go beyond' the modifications undergone by the objects and the varying qualities exhibited by it under different conditions. Whether we refer to the different modes of the object or to the diverse qualities of the object, the point of reference *is* to the *object itself*. But for the persistence of the object itself, expressions like 'changing modes' and 'differing qualities' will not be meaningful. The modes requiring a foundation and the qualities which need a 'support' are both evident. What needs to be noted here is that the description attempted is from the point of view of the object itself, or, in traditional metaphysical terms, from the viewpoint of Substance.

Another description of the same object is as follows: The object may be attempted to be understood also by dwelling on the various shapes or forms (i.e. modes) it has assumed and by the divergent qualities it exhibits. For a start, only the 'shapes' and 'qualities' might have been noticed. For all we know, these alone might have struck the attention of the observer who then analysed them and surmised that these shapes and qualities related to something. "These shapes are of something, these qualities too *belong to* some object', he might have inferred. He might even have concluded that the very understanding of these which he had perceived, depended on the objects that 'possessed' them. But for the objects which were beneath or behind the modes and qualities, the latter did not have a meaning of their own, he might continue, but emphasise, all the same, that he had a better understanding of the object itself, thanks to his dwelling at length on the modes and qualities. The second description, it is needless to state, has been made from the viewpoint of qualities. In metaphysical terms, the second is a description of modes and attributes.

The Jaina philosophers seem to argue that the very fact that the two descriptions made from two different points of view but of the *same object* might well indicate (especially since the two descriptions are reciprocally related to each other) that they all coexist and cohere in the same object.

The idea of persistence, they seem to argue, does not entail the rejection of the idea of change (in modes and qualities).

In this connection Matilal has made a significant observation, clarifying the Jaina standpoint on the issue. Drawing a distinction between *continuity* and *permanence*, he writes:

> The former notion means persistence...(*pravāhanityatā*). The latter notion means immutability. It is the notion in the back-ground of which the triple character of origination, destruction and continuity becomes meaningful. 'Continuity', on the other hand, is a notion essentially dependent upon origin and decay.[22]

In support, the observations of Kundakunda and his commentator are cited. Kundakunda's observation is as follows:

> There is no origin without destruction, nor is there any destruction without origin, and neither is destruction nor origination possible without what continues to be.[23]

The commentator Amṛtacandra Sūri explains the above statement with a simple example. If a pot is produced from a lump of clay, the persistence of the clay (substance) itself is made possible by the origin and destruction of the pot. He argues:

> If we do not accept it as true, origin, decay and continuity all three will then be really different from one another. In that case, when the mere origin of the pot is sought after, then either it will not originate for there will not be any (real) cause for its origin, or there will be the origination of the non-existent (an untenable paradox). If the pot does not originate, no bhāvas (things) will originate. If there is origination of the non-existent (asat), then the sky-flower etc. will come into being. Similarly, if mere destruction of the lump of clay is attempted (to the exclusion of the production of the pot), then either there will not be any destruction of the lump for want of any (real) cause for such destruction, or there will be destruction of the existent or being (another untenable position).[24]

This signifies that the complexity of the object is understandable in terms of the ideas of persistence as well as changes. No doubt, these terms *qua* terms, may be considered 'opposites' just as the two stand-points from which the description of the object is made may be considered *two* diametrically opposed ones.

It would emerge then that even when only one aspect, viz. the material aspect (*pudgala*) of *Ajīva* is considered, that too by restricting our focus on an aspect of the metaphysical problem of Substance (as we have done above), the Jaina view of the complexity of Reality becomes apparent. Add to that the inclusion of *dharma, adharma, ākāśa* and *kāla* (the principle of motion, the principle of rest, space and time),[25] the formless sub-categories of *Ajīva*, the main thesis of Jaina metaphysics becomes even more evident.[26]

Before proceeding further it should be stressed that the idea of manifoldness (*anekānta*) can be derived from the idea of the many (*anekata*) in so far as the many reals together would account for the complex nature of their relationship, even considered merely from the point of view of the *number of reals* and the corresponding multiplicity of relations into which the Reals enter. Visualising each one of the Reals as possessing a number of aspects either in terms of the *attributes* they have or in terms of the *modal changes* they undergo, or in terms of both attributes and modes they are 'endowed with', would strengthen rather than weaken the idea of *manifoldness*. The basic idea of *many* has thus been understood here in terms of the number of categories and sub-categories accepted by a system under consideration, Jainism itself not being an exception.

This is a clear pointer to the inevitable emergence of many schools of philosophy with the implication that to the extent that they all (the schools) have a common reference-point, they *all* represent several attempts at unravelling the complex significance of the underlying concept of Reality, the focal point of their analyses. This is not to *deny* the obvious, viz. that there are points of divergence between them but rather to *affirm* that there are *points of overlap*, these latter relating to Reality providing the subject-matter for the various perspectives themselves.

We have thus noted that despite the importance accorded to the manifoldness-aspect (*anekānta*) of Reality, the manyness-aspect (*anekata*) too deserves serious consideration while gauging the significance of *Anekāntavāda* for understanding the Jaina concept of philosophy. The cautious note we strike here is that in view of the centre-of-stage status usually given to the complex nature of Reality, the other idea, viz. that of divergent viewpoints emerging, is likely to be pushed to the background and consequently made to lose the foundational significance it actually possesses.

It seems to me therefore that the innate significance of the many-ness-idea needs to be specifically highlighted. My argument here is that the Jaina tradition does this by formulating the doctrine of *Nayavāda* (philosophy of perspectives). The importance of this doctrine has no doubt been acknowledged by some scholars by considering *Anekāntavāda* and *Syādvāda* as its two wings.[27] All the same, by reiterating the need for considering it *not* as an autonomous theory but as one which is of central importance, it is hoped that the deeper implications of *Anekāntavāda* itself for a concept of philosophy can be brought to the fore.

Nayavāda or Philosophy of Standpoints

The doctrine of *Nayavāda* may thus be looked upon as providing the framework for evolving a philosophy of philosophy (*meta philosophy*). This can be understood best by considering the idea of *perspectives*. A *naya* represents a *point of view* from which the nature of a thing is attempted to be comprehended. Since in regard to anything, many aspects can be visualised, the standpoints from which they are comprehended may also be deemed to be *many*. In this sense, the need to concede the existence of many standpoints and more importantly, their worthwhileness in revealing the nature of the thing under observation may both be reiterated.

The case cannot be different when the subject-matter of study is Reality. The variegated nature of Reality requires many different viewpoints from which it is analysed and understood. The many viewpoints here envisaged may even be considered infinite in number, - whether we deem the complex nature of Reality as possessed of an infinite number of qualities or enumerate the points of view that emerge when innumerable minds are at work to comprehend its multifaceted nature. In this sense, an infinite number of *nayas* may be thought of to be a distinct possibility. But the Jaina philosophers have indicated the situation of 'multiple possibilities' by mentioning more specifically, seven *nayas*.

What is interesting here is that these *nayas* enumerated are seen to comprehensively cover all the major metaphysical problems raised by philosophers the world over. If the various schools of Indian philosophy are envisaged as offering a comprehensive coverage of these major problems of metaphysics, and if the Jaina philosophers are seen as reacting critically to these various schools, it would appear that in and through their *Nayavāda* they have indicated the need for criticism in philosophy.

The import of such a theory is explicitly stated by one of the Jaina philosophers when he observes:

> All the standpoints (*nayas*) are valid from their respective angles - but if they are taken to be refutations, each of the other, they are wrong. But one who has comprehended the 'non-one-sided' nature of reality never considers a particular view absolutely wrong.[28]

Absolute refutations as much as absolute affirmations are unacceptable and hence are criticised. This idea emerges clearly from the fact that the focus of concern is shifted from the traditional seven-fold *nayas* to the basic division into the *dravyāstikanaya* (The Substance point of view) and the *paryāyāstikanaya* (The Modal Viewpoint). This is also in keeping with the dominant trend of thought in Jainism, viz. defining Reality as possessed of origination, destruction and permanence.[29] Such a definition of Reality from the Jaina side can well be seen as its critical response to the Brahmanical as well as the Buddhistic views. As against the Brahmanic portrayal of Reality as never-changing and as against the anti-thesis propogated by the Buddhists, viz. that Reality is ever- changing, the Jaina philosophers maintained that Reality is not merely permanent but it is equally well ever-changing. In this connection a Jaina scholar observes:

> It was an old Jaina poisition that *dharma, adharma,* ākāśa, souls and atoms are so many permanent substances but it was always conceded that all these substances possess properties that might come and go. (As for the composite physical substances, the position was that their constituent atoms are permanent even if they themselves must originate and perish.) It was in this background that one had to understand the ... contention that an atom, a soul (and) a *naraka* was permanent from the standpoint of *dravya* and transient from that of *paryāya* or *bhāva*.[30]

The *dravyanaya* and *paryāyanaya* were indicated earlier on in our discussion of Substance as representing the ideas of *Being* and *Becoming*. The critical reaction of the Jaina philosophers was not against the two ideas as such but rather against the two ideas being maintained exclusively, i.e. by excluding the 'other' idea. The indication clearly is that if a point of view (whether it is that of Being or that of Becoming) is proposed as the only valid one as against the claim of validity put forward by an opposed theory, it was not acceptable to the Jaina thinkers. Explaining the *rationale* of the Jaina theory of standpoints discernible here, S.N. Dasgupta writes:

> In framing judgments about things, there are two ways open to us. Firstly we may notice the manifold qualities and characteristics of anything but view them as unified in the thing; thus when we say "this is a book" we do not look at its characteristic qualities as being different from it, but rather the qualities or characteristics are perceived as having no separate existence from the thing. Secondly we may notice the qualities separately and regard the thing as a mere non-existent fiction (cf. the Buddhist view); thus I may speak of the different qualities of the book separately and hold that the qualities of the things are alone perceptible and the book apart from these cannot be found. These two points of view are respectively called *dravyanaya* and *paryāyanaya*.[31]

For our purposes it is important to note that this broad division of *nayas*, not to speak of the seven *nayas* subsumed under them, is of very ancient origin in the Jaina tradition; as such, the 'Standpoint Doctrine' may well be considered to suggest the considered Jaina view that critical analyses (of extreme positions) are vitally required in philosophy.

This is clear when the purport of the various *nayas* is analysed. What is significant here is that the need for criticism in philosophy suggested by the Jaina philosophers through *Nayavāda* is equally indicative of the prime importance that should be accorded to major problems of metaphysics; for, the critical assessments of different systems of philosophy identifiable in the different *nayas* and indicated below, are aimed at pointing to the major flaws in their basic metaphysical positions.

Naigamanaya (Universal-Particular Standpoint)[32]

The metaphysical problem raised here is the issue of Universals and Particulars. Notwithstanding the fact that the terms 'Universal' and 'Particular' are defined differently by philosophers of different persuasions and, despite the distinction which can be drawn between philosophers' views on these (on the basis of their epistemological positions), it cannot be gainsaid that there *is* an area of agreement between them on the fundamentals. For instance, the *particular* is understood as a 'specific instance', and the *Universal,* as something which characterises a number of 'specific particulars'. One of the burning problems in this area is regarding the nature of the relation between them, - more specifically finding out whether they could be distinguished from each other.

From the fact that when a complete description of an object (a 'particular') is attempted, the presence of a characteristic belonging to other objects (other 'particulars' of its kind) cannot but be conceded and the 'presence' of an 'universal' in it can thus be acknowledged, it may be surmised that the object, in some sense, incorporates within itself, both the universal and the particular. Though they *may be distinguished* for thought (i.e. for analytical purposes), they are, in reality, *not distinct.*

Among the schools of Indian philosophy, the Nyāya-Vaiśeṣika system is especially known for the distinction it draws between categories among which the universal (*sāmānya*) and particular (*viśeṣa*) are included. According to the Jaina philosophers, the Nyāya-Vaiśeṣikā philosophers commit a fallacy called *naigamābhāsa* since they maintain an absolute distinction (*atyantabhinnatva*) between the various categories they propose. The fallacy arises because the distinction is asserted *absolutely.*

The Jaina position is that though the distinction can be drawn, it is only *relative.* Even the non-distinction which is asserted, is not absolute. In this connection the Jaina definition of *naya* as a particular opinion (*abhiprāya* or *abhimata*) or a viewpoint (*apekṣa*) - a viewpoint which does not rule out other different viewpoints and is, thereby expressive of a partial truth (*vastvamsagrahi*) about an object (*vastu*) - as entertained by a knowing agent (*jñātr*)[33] is well worth remembering.

The upshot of the critical approach of the Jaina philosophers is that when one viewpoint (either of the universal or of the particular) is taken and the other (be it the particular or the universal) is set aside as irrelevant, a distorted picture of Reality emerges. Hence is the need for considering various viewpoints *in relation to* rather than *in contradistinction to*, one another.

Saṅgrahanaya (The Class Point of View)

The distinction between the *naya* which has just been considered and the present one is not clear on the surface. But on a careful study, the analytical approach of *Nayavāda* in general and the advance made in analysis by the *naya* under consideration in particular, comes to the fore.

When reference is made to *Naigamanaya*, the focus is kept on the idea of an object (any object) as holding within it an integrated network of the universal and the particular, - for instance, of 'treeness' (universal) and a specific tree (particular instance in which the universal finds expression). The *Saṅgrahanaya* revolves round the concept of *class-characteristic* (the genus) rather than a *particular kind* (the species). Reference to 'the tree' rather than specifying it as a 'mango tree' or a 'neem tree' represents the point of attention (required) in this *naya*. If 'that tree' is used as a reference-point, - for instance, to indicate the 'locale' an enquirer is not sure about - (to indicate that the house he is looking out for, is opposite 'that tree'), the idea of 'that tree' is more relevant and contextually more meaningful than 'that mango tree' or 'that neem tree', and to that extent, it obliterates (though for a time only) the two latter ones. This is *Saṅgrahanaya* pointed out as being concerned with the general or the class-character.[34]

It is important to note that though the concern here is with the genus, the species is not totally negated;[35] for, though attention is paid on 'that tree' as a reference-point, it is not denied that it is a 'mango tree' or 'neem tree' or any other kind of tree (as the case may be) inasmuch as 'that tree' must be one of the kind.

The fallacy which is likely to be committed here may well be visualised. It occurs when undue emphasis is laid on the class-characteristic, - taking no account of the species which falls under the genus. This is referred to as *saṅgrahābhāsa* or the 'fallacy of class' by the Jaina philosophers.

The Sāṅkhya school and the Advaita-Vedānta school are criticised by the Jaina philosophers as committing this fallacy. The former is taken to task for maintaining that only Substance exists.[36] The implication here seems to be that to the extent that *Prakṛti* (as one of the two main principles accepted by Sāṅkhya) is considered 'unmodified', extreme stress is laid on the 'one' rather than on the 'many', - on the genus rather than on the species. The charge against the latter is that in pronouncing everything as *Sat* (Existent), the *asat* (non-existent) aspect of Reality is completely overlooked. The Jaina view is that the proposition 'Everything is *sat*'[37] is intelligible only if the *asat*-aspect is temporarily shut out, i.e. only when its being a necessary complement of *sat* is not permanently ignored. The criticism against the Sāṅkhya and the Advaita schools is, in effect, a plea for considering *class* not as something opposed to or as something other than its constituent *members*. The class and its members should be understood in terms of each other.

Vyavahāranaya (The Empirical Standpoint)

When the term 'empirical' is mentioned, it is at once identified as being concerned with immediate experience, especially sensory experience. The more specific nature of this *naya* is especially evident when we recount the distinct feature of the previous *naya* as the 'general'.

The Class Point of View is more abstract in contradistinction to the empirical inasmuch as it is arrived at only as a result of abstracting a common quality (an universal characteristic) shared by a number of tangible, concrete objects given to us in our empirical experience. An analysis of what is empirically experienced and the need felt to 'go beyond' what is actually presented to the sense-organs result in identifying the class-characteristics. In this sense it may also be referred to as meta-physical since passing beyond the physical-actual is involved in arriving at the Class point of view.

The *Vyavahāranaya* is thus limited in scope since by definition it is not concerned with anything other than the 'actually given'. Empirical experience, as resulting from the response of the sense-organs to stimuli presented to them from the world immediately outside the experiencer cannot but have a narrow sphere of reference. But as a *naya*, this point of view does not assert that there is no need to go beyond sensory experience. All that is implied here is that dwelling on the given (sensory experiences) is a viewpoint which can and in fact, *is* oftentimes adopted, with its own advantages not the least of which is that it helps the process of inductively arriving at a common core. As such, ruling out the Class idea which is not given in sense-experience is not suggested at all.

Obviously therefore the Jaina philosophers were critical of the attitude of acquescing in what is given in sense-perception, in stubbornly refusing to concede that perception cannot be the only source of reliable knowledge regarding Reality. Though the reliability of sense-experience is not totally rejected, the outright rejection of the possibility of going beyond the given is unacceptable to it. Among the Indian schools of philosophy, the Cārvāka materialist philosophers are criticised by the Jaina philosophers as being totally committed to the empirical standpoint. This is responsible for their commiting the fallacy of *vyavahāranayābhāsa.*[38] Relying exclusively on empirical experience is considered fallacious since it shuts out totally the metaphysical Class point of view.

With the consideration of the above *naya* we have dealt with all the *nayas* collectively known as *dravyanayas* or the viewpoints which are concerned with the enduring aspect of Substance or Reality. The remaining four, the *paryāyanayas*, are concerned with the changing aspects of Reality. The first one of them alone needs to be considered here since it is more directly concerned with the metaphysical problem of change. This is *Ṛjusūtranaya*, the *viewpoint of momentariness.*

The need to concede the significance of the moment can hardly be denied. And the Jaina philosophers do not commit the mistake. They are rather wary of those like the Buddhists[39] who extol the significance of the moment and have built a whole philosophy of momentariness (*kṣaṇikavāda*) around it.

That the idea of change is as undeniable as the idea of persistence, has been a cardinal principle in Jaina metaphysics as we have been pointing out in some other contexts in this study. Doing metaphysics then cannot afford to shut out either of the aspects. While dwelling on the aspect of change may be an antedote to denying change altogether and focusing on the persistence-aspect of Reality may be deemed as counterbalancing the tendency to affirm the significance of change as an exclusive characteristic of Reality, relying on one of them and totally excluding the other is critically viewed by the Jaina philosophers.

Ṛjusūtranaya is intended to acknowledge the value of the standpoint of momentariness as one of the viewpoints which might help us understand Reality. This idea of change is not explicable unless the moments that constitute it are accepted as real. But this is to argue that the various moments put together would constitute Reality. What is meant is that the chain of continuity running through and relating the moments rather than moments *qua* moments, constitute Reality. The acceptance of the significance of moments does not (rather, should not) entail a denial of the idea of persistence as such. It rather means that considering moments is helpful in understanding continuity and persistence.

The Buddhists have, according to this line of thinking, overshot the mark by denying the value of standpoints other than that of moments: And to this extent, such a stand is to be regarded as one-sided and hence is not to be accepted absolutely. Relative acceptance of its claims rather than an absolute rejection of its counter-claims, is all that the Jaina philosophers could grant while reacting critically to such a view of momentariness. It is worth reiterating here that the Jaina philosophers adopted the same approach to other one-sided viewpoints, i.e. critically assessed the aspects (of those views) which could be accepted.

This brings us to a concluding observation regarding the Jaina philosophy of criticism in general and the significance of *Anekāntavāda* in particular. If critical reflection is considered an important aspect of philosophising in the Jaina tradition, as the brief survey of the various *nayas* has revealed, criticism is deemed necessary to be a "functional corrective" of the attitude of philosophers who have resorted to taking extreme positions and vehemently arguing that the positions taken rule out all other alternative standpoints.

The critical attitude taken by the Jaina philosophers against other schools of Indian philosophy in this regard and, by implication, - their advocating the need to scrutinise carefully the extremist viewpoints taken in philosophy - may then be described aptly as espousing a non-one-sided approach to problems in philosophy. *Anekāntavāda* may be understood as standing for not (*na*) a one-sided (*ekānta*) argument (*vāda*). It seems to say 'No' (*na*) to one-sided views (*ekāntavādas*). It may be interpreted as *countering* one-sided arguments.

But the expression 'countering one-sided arguments' and the point intended to be made have to be carefully understood. The countering of one-sided arguments suggested by *Anekāntavāda* is not in the spirit of putting them down in order to advance a counter-argument. *Anekāntavāda* which stands for an acceptance of aspects of many (*aneka*) views is not to be considered as an exact opposite of views which stand for specific, one-sided (*ekānta*) perspectives, as Matilal has noted.[40] For, the spirit of the doctrine requires that a one-sided view is *not rejected totally but accepted partially* with a view to synthesising it with other views.

In this sense it might be suggested that *Anekāntavāda*, as a critical method in philosophy, is ultimately concerned with arriving at a comprehensive picture of Reality, first by a process of *analysis* and then by a process of *synthesis*. The process of analysis has just been explicated by a consideration of *Nayavāda* and the process of synthesis is yet to be considered. We shall take this up in the next chapter.

Notes and References

1 See pp. 15-16

2 B.K. Matilal notes that Jaina philosophy unfolded itself in the context of many severe and serious controversies among such schools as the Sāṅkhya, Bauddha, Nyāya, Mīmāṁsā and Vedānta. He suggests that *Anekāntavāda* historically presupposes the existence of many rival and well-developed philosophical schools. *Vide The Central Philosophy of Jainism*, Ahmedabad: L.D. Institute of Indology, 1981, pp. 1-2.

3 See p. 12

4 See p. 18

5 Y.J. Padmarajiah, *Op. Cit.*, pp. 274-275.

6 Satkari Mookerjee, *The Jaina Philosophy of Non-Absolutism*, Calcutta : Bharati Mahavidyalaya Publications, Jaina Series no. 2, 1944, p. 70.

7 *Sarvārthasiddhi*, V. 25

8 Six forms of *Skandha* are recognised in Jainism. These are:

(i) *Bhadra-bhadra*: This type of *skandha*, when split, cannot regain the original, undivided form. Solids are typical examples.

(ii) *Bhadra*: When split, this type of *skandha* has the capacity to join together. Liquids are the examples cited.

(iii) *Bhadra-sūkṣma:* This type of *skandha* appears gross but is really subtle, as is evident from the fact that it can neither be split nor is capable of being pierced through or taken up in hand. Examples cited are: sun, heat, shadow, light, darkness, etc. Minute particles of these are evident to the senses.

(iv) *Sūkṣma-bhadra:* This type of *skandha* also appears gross but is also subtle. Examples cited are: sensations of touch, smell, colour and sound.

(v) & (vi) Both are extremely subtle and beyond sense-perception. The particles of *karma* are cited as examples. - See A Chakravarti, *Religion of Ahiṁsā*, Bombay: Ratanchand Hirachand, 1957, p. 117.

9 Regarding the Jaina theory of matter and space, M. Hiriyanna (*Outlines of Indian Philosophy*, London: George Allen & Unwin Ltd., 1931, p. 212 f.) comments as follows: "The atoms, according to it (Jainism) are all of the same kind, but they can yet give rise to the infinite variety of things so that matter as considered here is of quite an indefinite nature. *Pudgala* has, as we know, certain inalienable features, but within the limits imposed by them it can become anything through qualitative differentiations. The transmutation of elements is quite possible in this view and is not a mere dream of the alchemist."

10 *Dravya-Saṅgraha*, 19

11 See M.L. Metha, *Op. Cit.*, p. 34

12 *Ibid.*

13 Prabhācandra's *Nyāya-kumuda-candra*, a commentary on *Laghiyastraya* of Bhattakalanka, edt., Mahendrakumar Shastri, Manikchandra Digambar Jain Series, Bombay, 1938. (Cited in Padmarajiah, *Op. Cit.*, p. 283)

14 *Syādvādaratnākara*, 5 parts by Vadidevasuri, a commentary on *Pramāṇanayatattvālokālaṅkāra* by the same author. (Cited in Padmarajaiah, *ibid.*)

15 *Tattvārtha-Sūtra*, V. 30

16 See *Tattvārtha-bhāṣya*, V. 29

17 *Tattvārtha-Sūtra*, V. 37

18 *Ibid.*, V. 40

19 *Tattvārtha-bhāṣya*, V. 40

20 See *Pūjyapāda, Sarvārthasiddhi*, V. 38 (Cited in B.K. Matilal, *Op. Cit., pp. 35-36.*

21 Vedānta and Buddhism respectively espouse the ideas of *Being* and *Becoming*.

22 *Op. cit.*, p. 38

23 *Pravacanasāra*, II. 8

24 Commentary on *Pravacanasāra*, II. 8 (Cited in Matilal, *Op. Cit.*, p. 8)

25 *Tattvārthasāra*, V. 4

26 See the present author's *Outlines of Jainism*, 1973, pp. 133-144 for a more elaborate treatment.

27 See Padmarajaiah, *Op. Cit.*, p.

28 Siddhasena, *Sanmati-tarka*, I. 28

29 K.K.Dixit, *Jaina Ontology*, Ahmedabad: L.D. Institute of Indology, 1971, p. 90

30 *Ibid.*

31 *Op. Cit.*, Vol. I, pp. 76-77

32 Another meaning of this expression is "Teleological Standpoint," but in our context we can gloss over it. Our main interest here being metaphysics and the problems discussed under this sub-division of philosophy, we shall confine our attention to the problem of Universal alone here.

33 Padmarajaiah, *Op. Cit.*, p. 310

34 Vadidevasūri's commentary, *Syādvādaratnākara*, on *Pramāṇanayatattvālokālaṅkāra*, VII. 13 (Cited in Padmarajiah, *Ibid.*, p. 316.) See also *Tattvārtha- Śloka-vārttika*, 51, p. 270

35 Vinaya Vijaya, *Naya-karṇikā*. 6 (Cited in Padmarajiah *Ibid.*)

36 *Sanmatī-tarka*, III. 48

37 *Pramāṇanayatattvālokālaṅkāra*, VII. 16 (Cited in Padmarajiah, *Ibid.*, p. 317)

38 *Ibid.*, VII. 26 (Cited in *Ibid.*, p. 318)

39 It is significant to note that despite the fact that Jaina philosophers accorded an important place to change in their theory of Reality, they were not hesitant to take up issues with the Buddhists on the count that Reality has the dynamic as well as static aspects integrated in its structure.

Chapter Four
PHILOSOPHY AS CRITICISM - II

Before delineating further the idea of Jainism as *metaphilosophy* it is necessary to explicate further the significance of the *critical method* espoused by Jaina philosophers. The suggestion in the last chapter was that the need to adopt a critical method in philosophy was indicated in the Jaina tradition through two theories, *Anekāntavāda* and *Syādvāda*. Our endeavour in considering the first of these in some detail immediately as a follow-up of the suggestion was to indicate that the analytical procedure provides the critical method with a direction and a purpose. In the concluding part of that discussion it emerged that the critical method equally well required a complementary procedure of synthesis - this for reaching the destination by following the direction, i.e. for achieving the aim postulated for philosophy.

I want to spell out at this point that the idea of criticism espoused in Jainism is to be understood as constructive-positive rather than as destructive-negative. By the former expression is meant a creative approach to philosophy in which the value of the contribution of various schools is recognised and appreciated. Conversely the latter expression points to the attitude of putting down rival claims on the assumption that they do not promote the cause of philosophy. The Jaina philosophers' disapproving this approach would signify that criticisms of rival points of view ought not to be undertaken for their own sake. Criticisms are not to be considered as ends-in-themselves but only as *means*.

It might be added here that the danger inherent in looking upon the critical method in philosophy as solely being concerned with exposing the defects of various alternative positions consists in the fact that developing a sceptical attitude is a distinct possibility. As against this, viewing the critical approach as merely a means carries with it the advantage of considering the function of criticism as highlighting the *limitations* of theories proposed in philosophy. Spotlighting the limitations presupposes that the theories under criticism have their own value, however limited they may be. Not condemning rival theories as totally worthless is tantamount to considering them significant in some respect.

We are now in a position to argue that a constructive-critical approach results by adopting the positive rather than a negative attitude to sister-systems and rival philosophers. Such an approach to other systems and schools of thought which scrupulously avoids destructive criticism and carefully nurtures creativity, incorporates within itself both the processes of *analysis* and *synthesis* as components which complement one another.

While *analysis* is mainly aimed at isolating and separating divergent strains of thought which are found together as related, *synthesis* is concerned chiefly with finding a meaningful whole in the situation of relatedness of different elements, ideas, parts or aspects. Synthesis signifies something more difficult to achieve than reconciliation. For, the latter is aimed at merely removing conflicts between opposites whereas the former points to a 'new creation' - creating something new out of different things, ideas, etc. which need not necessarily be opposites of each other. Obviously therefore *reconciliation* by itself need not always pave the way to a synthesis just as attempts at arriving at a synthesis need not presuppose opposition and confrontation. Such a distinction need not preclude areas of overlap either. And it is because of this that the idea of synthesis can be understood better by considering the idea of reconciliation.

Reconciliation is sought after when the inquirer is faced with two opposite theories (S is P and S is not-P) regarding an issue (free-will, knowledge, existence of God, etc.). The attempt at reconciliation has been made in the history of philosophy in six different ways:[1]

1. By accepting one of the opposite theories as true and rejecting the other as false. (S is P; S is not not-P.) This type of reconciliation is quite common; it is resorted to frequently. It seems to be a natural tendency even among philosophers to resort to this method of reconciliation.

2 By partial acceptance and partial rejection of both theories. (Some S is P and Some S is not-P) An example from Descartes is: "Knowledge of external objects is due to sensation but knowledge of the Infinite is not so." An illustration from the Vaiśeṣika system is: "Change is real in regard to relations among ultimate elements but it is not so in respect of the elements themselves."

3 By accepting both the theories through a recognition of the complementary type of relationship between certain important aspects of them. (Every S is both P and Not-P in different but inseparable respects.) Kant's attempting to reconcile the claims of empiricism and Rationalism is a typical instance of this type of reconciliation; the role of the sense-organs in receiving sensations and the role of the mind in organising and interpreting them are both considered necessary, as useful complements in explaining the origin of knowledge. Reconciling the claims of determinism and freedom by pointing to the act of will as determined *by the self* and *not by factors external to oneself* is another instance.

4 By rejecting both (S is neither P nor not-P) on the count that the theories rest on a common wrong presupposition, the corrected version is proposed as a new theory. Henry Bergson's rejecting the theories of mechanism as well as finalism by the setting aside presupposition of predetermination and proposing the theory of creative evolution in their place illustrates this type of reconciliation.

5 By rejecting the underlying problem itself either as illegitimate (as Kant does in respect of questions like "Is the thing-in-itself one or many?") or as meaningless (as logical positivists do regarding metaphysical questions in general) or as undecidable (as the Buddha does in regard to questions like "Is the world eternal?") or as self-contradictory (as Śaṅkara does regarding the question "Do I exist?").

6 And lastly, by conceding the limitations of the rational faculty in man and admitting the superiority of intuitive experience. Reconciling the claims of reason and intuition by relegating the former to the empirical realm and considering the latter to be ultimately effective in reaching the transcecendental level is frequently witnessed in western as well as eastern philosophy. In the West Bradley's replacing the sphere of Appearance by resorting to immediate pure experience is a good instance. The ideas of *Śūnya* and *Ātman* resulting from the dialectical arguments of Nāgārjuna and Śriharṣa are illustrations of this way of reconciliation from the side of eastern philosophy.

It is obvious how only two of the above are capable of enabling the inquirer to arrive at a synthesis, viz. the second and the third. It is only in them that some elements of the conflicting theories are retained and if carefully handled, both the ways of reconciliation can be made to result in the emergence of something new. And the focus of the Jaina philosophers was precisely on these two ways of 'reconciling' the claims and counter-claims of divergent systems of philosophy. The reason for this type of approach to the problem of reconciliation (which has actually led to the process of synthesis) is worthwhile analysing here.

Needless to say, we should not visualise the Jaina philosophers as having been concerned with the problem of choosing one or more of the various methods of reconciliation. References to the divergent ways in which solutions to problems of philosophy have been attempted represent our *reviewing* methods employed by philosophers whenever necessary. We consider such a philosophical stock-taking useful in the context of our analysis of the Jaina approach to problems. Hence the type of synthesis the Jaina philosophers aimed at is *not* to be construed as having resulted from their deliberately "wanting to create something new" from out of the various theories prevalent then but rather as a *natural sequel* to their attempting to indicate the manifold nature of Reality. That is, notwithstanding the fact that the Jaina philosophers were appreciative of the *need* for analysis, they were equally well aware of the limitations of considering analysis as an autonomous procedure in philosophy. The logical implication of such an approach to *analysis* was that it needed to be followed by a process of synthesis which would put together (not mechanically but in the organic sense of finding the rightful and reciprocal relationships between parts) the results of analysis. The Jaina philosophers' conceding the positive contributions of the various systems of philosophy was thus a result of their considering them significant in the effort at understanding Reality.

The different types of emphasis found in the *Nayavāda* which was analysed in the last chapter and the *Syādvāda* which is to be studied in the present chapter now becomes evident. Having already noted[2] that they are two different but closely related aspects of *Anekāntavāda* it now emerges that while the former lays its emphasis on *analysis*, the latter stresses the significance of *synthesis*.

The close-knit relationship between analysis and synthesis is presupposed in the doctrine of *naya* (*Nayavāda*) itself, no doubt since it highlights the need for considering the significance of other standpoints even when one standpoint is espoused. It is worth reiterating that fallacies (*nayābhāsas*) arise when the need to consider 'other views' is ignored.[3] But the doctrine of *Syāt* (*Syādvāda* or Maybeism), by pointing to the need for considering the various viewpoints *as together contributing to our knowledge of Reality*, clearly indicates that the process of understanding becomes complete only when the various views are considered in relation to one another. Far from reading contradictory doctrines into the divergent viewpoints, the Jaina thinkers have, in their *Syādvāda*, attempted to indicate that if carefully considered, the conflicts between divergent doctrines would be seen to be *seeming* rather than *real*. Since they are *not* inherently *irreconcilable*, the process of reconciliation suggested is not an artificially contrived one but is one that the diverse viewpoints themselves warrant.

The first step in indicating reconcilability is to suggest that extreme caution is to be observed in presenting viewpoints. This caution is to be observed particularly while formulating propositions to indicate different approaches to the nature of Reality. This seems to be the implication of a Jaina monk being required to take care of his speech.[4] He is prohibited against indulging in categorical assertions or negations.[5] A wise man should not mock at others, nor should he espouse his views without qualifying them.[6] He should explain, with the help of *vibhajya-vāda* and using conditional expressions.[7] Since the suggestion here is using non-categorical, qualified statements, the non-absolutist approach of the Jaina philosophers is clear. It is significant that the Jaina theory of *Anekānta* itself has been referred to as a non-absolutist theory of Reality as has been noted earlier.[8] It also needs to be noted here that in the method of seven-fold predication (*saptabhaṅgīnaya*),[9] absolute affirmation as well as categorical denial of statements concerning Reality are carefully avoided. The implications of both for a constructive-critical method in philosophy pleaded for by Jaina philosophers also deserve notice.

The Vibhajya method has been noted by researchers in Jainology[10] as one which was used both by the Buddha and Mahāvīra to tackle difficult metaphysical problems but in different ways and correspondingly with different effects, - these relating to the ways in which conflicts between opposite viewpoints could be resolved.

Interested as we are in the Jaina approach which was greatly inflenced by Mahāvīra's using the *vibhajya* method to espouse the theory of non-Absolutism, it is worth noting that it essentially involved the position that if there are different doctrines, there must be *reasons* for their diverse perspectives. It is the duty of a thinker to find out the sources of these doctrines.[11] The thinker should not be prejudiced by preconceptions but be always prepared to keep an open mind which would attempt to understand the reasons for the differences of opinion and conflicts of viewpoints. By adopting such a method, even doctrines which are generally considered to be totally opposed to one another and theories regarded as 'irreconcilable' and problems deemed irresoluble could be shown to be *reconcilable*, after all.

It would thus be seen that Mahāvīra was pleading for a radical *change of attitude* in regard to absolutistic notions on the count that our thoughts are *relative* and correspondingly too, our verbal expressions, - our articulations of thoughts in the form of propositions. This line of thinking was responsible for the view that Reality in its fullness cannot be grasped by relative thought and described completely by any proposition. The metho of doing philosophy can thus be seen here to be the concern of Mahāvīra. The expression "doing philosophy" is here to be uderstood[12] as indicating the way of approach to divergent theories proposed by different systems of philosophy.

It is indeed contextually significant to digress a little to take account of what is happening in the philosophic scene even today, for that would help us understand the Jaina concept of philosophy as criticism better. Today one of the important things that a philosopher does is to review critically other theories prevalent or even those which were proposed in the past (either in the immediate past or even in the remote past); this is the well-acknowledged, popularly accepted, method of recording a philosopher's reactions to other theories. The reactions are by way of accepting them and finding in them support for one's own views, if the thinkers reviewed belonged to the "same school" as the reviewer. The 'reviews' might result in rejecting positions or finding flaws in the arguments if the philosophers under review[13] belonged to a "different school" (quite often, to an 'opposed school of thought').

Indeed it is not an exaggeration to state that wherever philosophies have emerged, wherever systems of philosophy have flourished, wherever philosophical problems have been subjected to continuing discussions, we find philosophers grouping themselves into different schools. Affiliation to the divergent schools have invariably also meant owing allegiance to them. Commitments to certain basic tenets have resulted in virulent criticisms as well as strong condemnations of those schools, thinkers or proponents who have no such commitments. Accepting certain fundamental positions has had the effect of defending them against criticisms and also of looking out for loop-holes in the critics' positions.

Division of philosophers in the sense indicated has had a divisive effect inasmuch as their work has not been considered to have been conducive to the development of a coherent structure of thought but as having contributed, - though imperceptibly, to the emergence of sharply divided points of view. By the very nature of the stance they have *all* taken from the commencement of their inquiries, the prospects of 'reconciliation' not to speak of 'synthesis' seem t have been bleak. The hopelessness of the situation is that possibilities of different schools working in harmony and for a common purpose (of pursuing the aim of philosophy) seem to get ruled out altogether, thanks to the enthusiasm with which specific standpoints are taken and the vehemence with which they are defended.

Such developments in the philosophic scene have been time and again subjected to critical reviews and these have led to meta-philosophical trends explicitly coming out with statements in regard to the way philosophies and philosophers should proceed or indicate, by implication, the pitfalls to be avoided by leaders of thought.

The spirit of the *vibhajya* method adopted by Mahāvīra is now easy to discern. Mahāvīra seems to point out that a dispassionate observation and a careful analysis of the so-called opposed schools of thought would indicate that if many points of view *have* been taken, if emphases have been laid on come ideas *as against* others, development of diverse perspectives *could not be helped*. Rather than analysing the situation as holding within it no potential for reconciliation and portending interminable controversies and polemics, Mahāvīra seems to have assessed the situation as quite promising. He seems to have found scope for viewing them all as together contributing to the enrichment of our knowledge of Reality.

It seems to me that such an approach discernible in Mahāvīra's *Vibhajya* method is a clear reflection of the basic Indian view that attachment (*rāga*) and aversion (*dveṣa*) both hamper the development of a philosophic view of life which, in the ultimate analysis, entails an open-minded approach. The development of such an approach would have a transforming influence on life and would reflect itself in every endeavour, not the least of which is considering the merits and demerits of various schools of thought. This point needs specific mention here since we are primarily interested in getting at the *rationale* behind Mahāvīra's method of constructive criticism as necessary and valuable.

The *Vibhajya* method would then involve, as Matilal suggests[14] the processes of analysing a question and its various presuppositions as also distinguishing between possible interpretations (and the term *vibhaga* is highly suggestive of these ideas); it signifies further the method of breaking up the whole (*vibhajya*) into its component parts.

The Jaina view that the various systems of philosophy are nothing but different approaches to Reality can then be seen as resulting from the recognition of the need for *analysis*. But since analysis as conceived here is with a view to understanding the whole, i.e. since analysis is not considered valuable in itself but as only one aspect of *doing philosophy*, the need for synthesis immediately suggests itself. The significance of synthesising the various views laid bare by a process of analysis also comes tothe fore. It is also suggestive of the idea that analysis without synthesis is as meaningless as considering synthesis as all-important by ignoring the role of analysis altogether.

In the Jaina tradition, the need for an analytical-synthetic approach to Reality has been explicated in the theory of manifoldness of Reality (*Anekāntavāda*) the details of which were outlined and interpreted in Chapter 3 of the present study. It was suggested then that *Nayavāda* and *Syādvāda* stand respectively for the procedures of *analysis* and *synthesis*. The philosophy of criticism found incorporated in these sub-doctrines was highlighted to argue for the metaphilosophical significance of the parent-doctrine, *Anekāntavāda*. The sub-doctrine of *Nayavāda* was analysed, towards the concluding part of that chapter to explicate the *idea of anaylsis as criticism*. Before delineating the detials of the other offshoot, *Syādvāda* in the concluding part of the present chapter, it is necessary to indicate how the philosophy of criticism takes a slightly different form in it.

What needs to be brought out in regard to *Syādvāda* is the *idea of synthesis as criticism.* The subtlety of this idea of criticism needs to be reiterated to indicate that *Syādvāda* complements *Nayavāda* by bringing to the fore the necessity to bring together various analytical perspectives derived through *Nayavāda*.

Starting with the idea that *analysis* and *synthesis* represent but two complementary aspects of philosophising, the argument could be advanced further by stating that (i) the procedure of synthesis completes the work of analysis and hence (ii) the idea of synthesis, despite the fact that it is taken up for consideration as 'another aspect', should not be considered distinct. In the overall treatment of philosophy as criticism, *Syādvāda* can be visualised only as criticism aimed at synthesising several one-sided doctrines.

Focusing our attention on (i) referred to above : *Syādvāda* emphasises positively the need for accepting the truth-claims of 'rival theories' with the method of conditional predication. Conditional acceptance of various theories signifies that they *all* have to be accepted, but not in the form of categorical formulations with which they have been presented. The critical method adopted in *Syādvāda* then is by accepting the contributions of different schools of thought even while rejecting their simple, categorical assertions or denial.[15] Such an adoption of the critical method is to be contrasted with the one involved in *Nayavāda* where the presentation of one-sided doctrines is first rejected and then they are all accepted as forming part of a 'confluence of perspectives', i.e. as non-one-sided presentations.

It is easy to see how the point made in (ii) above follows as a necessary corollary. Synthesising different points of view is not possible unless the latter are considered only as *aspects* of a totality. As long as the different perspectives are considered as independent viewpoints which claim validity for themselves as against other perspectives, no meaningful synthesis can result. But the moment they are recognised as points of view which have been proposed from different angles and hence as valid only from the respectives spheres of vision, synthesis as a distinct possibility emerges. This is because the function of synthesis as consisting in bringing together the different aspects of a discussion is facilitated by each view bringing in its own contribution from its own angle.

The idea of criticism espoused by the Jaina tradition in *Syādvāda* then may be understood as being born out of the observation that divergent schools of thought proceed on the uncriticial assumption that there is absolutely nothing in the 'other schools' which deserved consideration. In view of this it is not surprising that they are highly critical of each other and indulge in polemics, —throwing away valuable viewpoints and writing off whole schools of philosophy. It looks as if schools of philosophy have inadvertently taken on themselves mainly two functions, viz. *formulating certain propositions concerning Reality* and *coming out with tirades against others* which offer alternative points of view.

Metaphilosophical considerations weighing with Jainism perhaps resulted in asking the more fundamental question as to why schools of philosophy should vary so much in their visions of Reality and coming out with the answer that Reality being complex in its complexion and structure was responsible for the emergence of divergent, critical and uncompromising stances. Formulating simple, categorical propositions on the nature of Reality, as the various schools did, was hence unacceptable to Jainism.

When the situation of mutually recriminatory viewpoints characterising philosophical speculation is analysed, three possibilities suggest themselves :

(a) All viewpoints may be totally wrong;

(b) Some viewpoints may be wrong and others, right; and

(c) All viewpoints may be right.

Jainism seems to have rejected the first alternative on the count that it would lead to agnosticism, and the second, on the ground that it was also a case of indulging in categorical assertions and denials. The third was acceptable for the reason that it made for the attitude of considering all viewpoints as worthwhile analysing. Obviously the viewpoints being but different perspectives which have been brought in, could not be unconditionally accepted. They could be accepted with the important provision that the acceptance of the one did not necessarily entail the rejection of other views, simply because they were 'other views'. And also because, *ex hypothesi*, they were made from divergent standpoints. In their *Syādvāda* theory the Jainas devised a way of avoiding categorical references by qualifying every possible proposition with the expression '*Syāt*' which means "May be". The conditional acceptance accorded to various propositions deserves to be described as an attempt at synthesising various viewpoints taken and propositions arrived at, consequent on the adoption of the analytical procedure earlier on.

Though the complexity of Reality is well indicated by formulating seven propositions,[16]—all with the qualifying *Syāt* particle, the Jaina philosophers, by referring to four factors, viz. substance (*dravya*), place (*kṣetra*), time (*kāla*) and mode (*paryāya*) seem to have indicated a many-pronged attack on the problem of unravelling the nature of Reality.

A brief consideration of these would be helpful in understanding the idea both of the complexity of Reality and the idea of conditional lpredication. The idea of complexity is indicated by suggesting that for a complete description of Reality all the four factors are to be referred to and the conditional predication idea is underlined by the insistence that the factor under consideration is only one among various alternatives to be considered.

We shall take up the example of pot (*ghata*) to explain the four factors. The existence of the pot first and foremost connotes its being made of some substance,—whatever it may be—so that a positive statement derives its meaning only from the point of view of the substance of which the pot is actually made and from no other viewpoint. The description, "The pot is made of mud" would be meaningful *only if* the substance used is mud, not if it is made of any other substance,—copper, silver. gold, etc.

Similarly the pot's existence can be affirmed from the point of view of the place in which it exists and not when it is not in that place. Suppose the pot is kept on the table here. When the pot is here, on the table, it cannot be elsewhere when reference is made to the existence of the pot, *in the context of the reference*, not to its absence anywhere else. The non-existence of the pot in other places may be *implied*, but when its existence is asserted, the reference is to the place where it actually exists. Where it does not exist, this proposition becomes invalid. The meaningfulness of the proposition concerning the pot's existence is thus contingent on its reference to its presence on the table. On the other hand, the validity of the proposition would be denied if the pot is pronounced as being present in a place where it is not. If I go to a place where the pot does not exist and say: "The pot exists here", I might be accused of giving expression to a meaningless proposition, just as it would be an invalid statement if I now say" "The pot does not exist here" eventhough the pot is present here.

Likewise we may visualise the time of existence of the pot. The pot exists *now* on the table. But suppose I inadvertently made it fall down and break to pieces. The pot no longer exists, i.e. the same pot which *existed* some time back, has actually gone out of existence. Hence the proposition which asserts the existence of the pot now becomes meaningless. The meaningfulness and the meaninglessness of the proposition are derived respectively from its *presence* and *absence* at the time the proposition is given expression to. So the time at which the object exists is an important consideration for validating the proposition under discussion. The pot did not exist till the moment it was made. Nor does it exist after it is broken. The validity of the proposition asserting the pot's existence correspondingly relates *only* to the period during which it really exists, not to the period before it came into existence nor to the period after it went out of existence.

The last factor, the modal factor, may be explained thus. 'Pot', as a term of reference, points to the shape given to a lump of clay by the potter. Only a specific shape that the potter, with the dexterity of his hands, has given to the clay, deserves such a description, *all other shapes* deserving oter descriptions. If a pot's shape is given, 'existence' refers to this specific mode, and hence the truth-value of the proposition is derived from this specific mode of existence of clay and not from that of any other.

Now we are in a position to explain the significance of the seven propositions (all with a qualifying clause, "May be") formulated as the *Syādvāda* doctrine.

The seven propositions are seven modes of predication and these are :

1 May be, Reality is (*Syāt asti dravyaṁ*)
2 May be, Reality is not (*Syāt nāsti dravyaṁ*)
3 May be, Reality is and is not (*Syāt asti ca nāsti ca dravyam*)
4 May be, Reality is indescribable (*Syāt avaktavyam* dravyaṁ)
5 May be, Reality is and is indescribable (*Syāt asti ca avaktavyam dravyaṁ*)
6 May be, Reality is not and is indescribable (*Syāt nāsti ca avaktavyam dravyaṁ*)
7 May be, Reality is, is not and is indescribable (*Syāt asti ca nāsti ca avaktavyaṁ dravyaṁ*)

In regard to the significance of this doctrine, S. Radhakrishan observes :

> It is the use in seven different ways of judgments which affirm and negate, severally and jointly, without self- contradiction, thus discriminating the several qualities of a thing. The difficulty of predication is got over in the Jaina theory, since it holds that subject and predicate are identical from the point of view of substance and different from the point of view of modification.[17]

In our terms : the emphasis on the idea of synthesis laid in the Jaina theory of *Syādvāda* is to be understood in terms of using affirmative as well as negative propositions to describe Reality without suggesting that from a synoptic point of view, affirmations and negations need not be considered contradictories. The affirmative ad negative forms can be deemed to lay contradictory claims only if they are categorically and unconditionally presented. Since the characteristic feature of presenting the 'claims' and 'counter-claims' in Jainism is by prefixing them with a "May be" (*Syāt*), it is obvious how the Jaina philosophers suggested a non-categorical, conditional formulation of the propositions.

The implicit criticism of Jainism against schools of philosophy which have resorted to taking the 'either-or method' (either affirming categorically or denying outright a viewpoint, as for instance, "Reality is ever-existing without changing" or "Reality is ever-changing without a semblance of identity") is that in the very process of *affirmation* (of one point of view) there is an act of *denial* (of other viewpoints). The corrective applied by Jainism is that by a conditional affirmation, the other viewpoint could also be accomodated not in a condescending manner but in a genuinely-felt, constructively thought-out positively-oriented, effort at comprehending the nature of Reality from many different perspectives which coalesce. This has resulted in prefixing the expression "May be" to the several propositions.

It seems therefore that the qualifying prefix is suggestive of the Jaina view that even when one viewpoint is put forward, asserted or accepted, it should not shut out the possibility of other views being put forward, other standpoints being asserted or other perspectives being conceded. The qualified statement ("May be, is", "May be, is not", etc.) brings to the fore, alternative possibilities; it suggests unequivocally that other standpoints *are* possible. Furthermore, the qualified acceptance (or denial) which the prefix of "May be" indicates is neither absolutely false nor totally true. Though acceptance of the validity of the proposition is indicated, what is not suggested is its total validity, just as the rejection of the soundness of the proposition is only on the count that an unconditional acceptance of validity might distort the nature of Reality. Dasgupta succinctly brings out the conditional affirmation aspect of the theory (explained above) thus :

> Infinite number of affirmations may be made of things from infinite points of view. Affirmations or judgments according to any naya or standpoint cannot therefore be absolute, for even contrary affirmations of the very . . . same things may be held to be true from other points of view. The truth of each affirmation is thus only conditional, and inconceivable from the absolute point of view. To guarantee correctness therefore each affirmation should be preceded by the phrase *syāt* (may be). This will indicate that the affirmation is only relative, made somehow, from some point of view, and under some reservations and not in any sense absolute. There is no judgment which is absolutely true, and no judgment which is absolutely false. All judgments are true in some sense and false in another.[18]

Passing on to a specific consideration of the seven propositions then, the following points emerge :

1 The proposition "Reality is", is to be understood as indicating existence in so far as this statement derives its validity from the point of view of *one* of the four factors indicated above, viz *substance, place, time* or *mode*. If the case of 'pot' is used as an instance of Reality as do the Jaina philosophers, the proposition "The pot is" is indicative of the *affirmation* of a particular substance of which the pot is made, the presence (of the pot) at the place at which it exists, the existence (of the pot) at the time at which the proposition is given expression to or the particular mode in which the pot is found. The affirmation cannot be unconditional since it derives its meaning only from the perspective of one of the four factors which is under consideration and from no other. Wshen the universe of discourse is the substance of which the pot is made, the proposition "The pot is" signifies existence of clay-pot if it *is* made of clay. If not, the proposition loses its validity.

2 The proposition "Reality is not" is not to be understood as indicating non-existence simultaneously since what is denied by the proposition is, in terms of the example, the pot being made of a different substance, its absence in another place (where it is not), its non-existence at a different point of time (at which it has either not yet come into existence or it has already gone out of existence) and a different mode of existence altogether, other modes of existence being named differently, i.e. as something else than pot.

The present proposition is not a contradictory of the first one since what is not denied here does not refer to the same factor which was asserted earlier on. The clay-pot's existence is not simultaneously affirmed and denied. What is denied is that the pot is made of a different substance. The implication is that if the pot is made of clay, any other affirmation that the pot is made of some other substance deserves to be negated. The present lproposition can also be interpreted along similar lines from the points of view of the other three factors, viz. place, time and mode.

3 The proposition "Reality is and is not" is then to be understood as not affirming and denying,—in terms of the clay-pot example—that the pot is made and is not made of clay *at the same time*. While the validity of the first part of this proposition is derived from the assertion that the pot *is* made of clay, the meaningfulness of the second part of the proposition stems from the denial of the fact that it is made of a different substance.

The present proposition may hence be regarded as advancing the arguments contained in propositions 1 and 2 in so far as the assertion that the pot *is* made of clay and denial, subsequently that it is *not* made of clay, are quite meaningful. While proposition 1 asserts that the pot is made of clay and proposition 2 denies that it is made of some other substance, proposition 3 explicitly points to the fact that a successive assertion (that the pot is made of clay) and denial (that the pot is not made of any other substance) *is*possible. In more concrete terms, the proposition is to be understood, in terms of our example, that the pot is made of clay and no other substance.

4 The proposition "The pot is indescribable" points to the situation where a simultaneous assertion that the pot is made of clay and a denial that it is not made of any other substance is attempted. The situation is one of indescribability or inexpressibility.

Logically it is impossible to describe meaningfully or express intelligibly the idea that the pot *is* made of clay and is *not* made of any other substance, at the same time. No doubt, the assertion that the pot is made of clay carries with it the implication that it is not made of any other substance. But it needs explication. A simultaneous explication of both ideas, if attempted, is found to be impossible. It is in this sense that the expression 'indescribability' is to be understood.

Psychologically too it is impossible to conceive of the two ideas, viz. that the pot *is* made of clay and *is not* made of a different substance *simultaneously*. Perhaps it is because of this psychological limitation that a verbal expression of both the ideas at one shot is not possible.

Hence this proposition is not to be understood as signifying that no description of the pot is possible, since a successive description of the basic substance of which it is made and of the substance of which it is not made is still possible. As Datta and Chatterjee point out :

> under such circumstances when we are forced to predicate simultaneously, of any object, characters which are incompatible, being contrary or contradictory, our judgment, according to the Jainas, would be of the general form "Somehow S is indescribable."[19]

We might also maintain that the recognition of this form of judgment shows that Jaina logic does not violate the principle of contradiction and that this is responsible for man's inability to simultaneously predicate incompatible characters of any subject from the point of view of the same factor.[20]

The remaining three propositions result from successively combining each of the first three propositions with the fourth. This exercise seems to give us an exhaustive description of Reality, for *Syādvāda* as emphasising the idea of synthesis is, by the very spirit of its method, *not* to leave the description incomplete—giving positive descriptions merely, making available negative descriptions alone or even by simultaneously describing Reality in positive as well as negative terms. It should also include the successive combinations of such descriptions of the various attempts at comprehending Reality.

5 The proposition "Reality is and is indescribable" is obtained by combining propositions 1 and 4. In terms of our example, when the proposition "The pot is made of clay" and "The pot is indescribable" are combined, the idea reiterated is this. The first part of the proposition points to the situation of describability of the substance of which the pot is made and the second part, to its indescribability when the substances of which the pot is and is not made are simultaneously attempted to be described.

6 The proposition "Reality is not and is indescribable", on analysis, reveals the *rationale* behind combining propositions 2 and 4 : *Des-cribability* signifies not merely stating positively that the particular object under consideration is made of a specific substance but also negatively stating that it is not made of any other substance. All the same, if this negative description is simultaneously attempted to be combined with a positive description, the situation of *indescribability* would be inevitable.

7 The proposition "Reality is, is not and is indescribable" reiterates further that propositions 1 and 2 can be meaningfully expressed if they are aimed at giving a positive and a negative description of the substance (of which the pot is made—in the example cited) successively. That is, if a positive and then a negative description is attempted, it would be successful in so far as either a positive or a negative description would result. On the other hand, if a simultaneous description—in positive and

negative terms—is attempted, the attempt would be clearly unsuccessful. This is the significance of the combination of the fourth proposition with the first and the second.

Before concluding this chapter, the significance of the non-absolutistic nature of propositions which attempt to describe Reality needs to be reiterated. The Jaina tradition holds that no categorical description of Reality, be it of the positive, affirmative type or the negative, denying type, is justifiable; for each description is true in some sense or the other. Each has validity in a limited sense only, and any of the seven alternatives referred to above would hold good in regard to every type of description.[21]

It is on this basis that Jainism is critical of the categorical nature of the standpoints taken by other Indian systems of philosophy. For one thing, these systems do not realise that an assertion can at best be conditional,—holding good only under certain circumstances or from the viewpoint of one of several factors which deserve attention, analysis and reflection. Universal validity as well as absolute invalidity of any of the propositions proposed would be seen to be not possible. For, inapplicability or applicability, meaninglessness or meaningfulness, in a different sense (i.e. other than what is proposed) and from a different perspective could be 'claimed' in respect of all viewpoints taken. Add to that the fact that Being and Becoming and Identity and Change (in the sense respectively of persistence and continuity) are observable empirically , the futility of absolutely affirming the validity of any proposition as well as wholly countering the affirmation would become clearer still.

Jainism as critical philosophy then would lay the claim for observing the principle of non-one-sidedness (*anekānta*) as follows: While taking different viewpoints (*naya*) is necessary for an analytical consideration of the nature of Reality, the very same procedure becomes fallacious if other viewpoints are not considered alongside the one adopted as required by the *Syādvāda* doctrine, for then the complementay procedure of synthesis would not have been observed and hence only an incomplete picture of Reality would have emerged. The aim of philosophy is thus to critically evaluate and constructively accept the results obtained by both procedures of analysis and synthesis.

Notes and References

1 See D.M. Datta, *Philosophical Perspectives*, Patna: Bharati Bhawan, 1972, pp. 25-26.

2 See *sūpra.*, p.18 where the idea was suggested in an implict form.

3 See *sūpra.*, pp. 37-43

4 *Ācāranga-Sūtra*, II. 4

5 *Ibid.*, II. 4. 1 and commentary.

6 *Sūtrakṛtāṅga*, I. 14. 19

It is obvious how the need to avoid the tone of sarcasm while presenting othe rviewpoints is exhorted here. The suggestion seems to be that due care should be taken while referring to other views and extreme caution should be observed while presenting one's own view. The tendency to understate the others' case and overstate one's own should be curbed.

7 *Sūtṛakrtaṅga*, I. 14. 22

8 see *sūpra.*, pp. 42-43 where the tirade against one-sided views was highlighted.

9 It will be seen that the basic idea here goes well with that in the theory of manifoldness.

10 Nathmal Tatia, *Op.Cit.* and B.K. Matilal, *Op.Cit.*

11 Tatia, *Ibid.*, p. 22

12 The other meaning, as we have noted (see *sūpra.*, pp. 27-28) relates to the subject-matter itself, more especially to constructing theories of Reality.

13 This is not to ignore the fact that the philosophic scene reveals a much more complicated reaction-pattern than has been portrayed here. It is rather to make the point that reactions generally tend towards either *acceptance* or *rejection* of theories different from those of the critic. If the reviewer and the reviewee subscribe to the same position, the reaction might be one of acceptance, but if they do not hold the same position, the reaction might be one of rejection. The case was not different in ancient India; nor is it different in the contemporary Indian philosophical scene.

14 *Op. Cit.*, p. 8

15 The subtlety involved in the critical method adopted by Jainism significantly reflects the complementary type of relationship that

is discernible in the processes of *analysis* and *synthesis*. Just as *analysis* and *synthesis* are not opposed processes but complement one another to enable a meaningful philosophical position to emerge, the attitudes of *acceptance* and *rejection* too need not be looked down upon as diametrically opposed procedures. They should rather be looked up to for arriving at a balanced picture of Reality by adopting the critical method in a creative-constructive way.

16. See *infra*., p. 58.
17. *Op. Cit.*, Vol. II, p. 302.
18. *Op. Cit.*, Vol. I, pp. 178-179.
19. *An Introduction to Indian Philosophy*, Calcutta : University of Calcutta, 1963 (first published, 1939), p. 84.
20. *Ibid.*
21. *Syādvādamañjarī, Hemacandra's commentary, p. 166.*

Chapter Five

CONCLUDING OBSERVATIONS

Before concluding this study of the concept of philosophy discernible in the Jaina tradition I deem it necessary to indicate the broad lines of argument presented in the preceding pages. Rather than merely summarising the viewpoint taken, I propose to highlight the significance of certain considerations which are crucial to an understanding of the Jaina view of philosophy.

The very title, *Jainism as Metaphilosophy*, would perhaps have indicated that the study undertaken has been aimed at indicating the contribution of this ancient Indian tradition to the on-going discussion concerning the aim, method, subject-matter and scope of philosophy. Obviously we have had to reconstruct the argument from the Jaina angle to seek to find an answer to the question : "How can the scope of philosophy be defined ?" The main reason for the restructuring has been that unlike us (the 'moderns') who are involved in the discussion, the ancient Indian philosophers were *not primarily concerned with the question* in so far as philosophy was not considered an academic study merely. All the same, the concepts characterising their systems *have* provided us with the grist for our discussion. It has thus involved some interpretation of the concepts by visualising the rationale behind the concepts themselves. The concept of philosophy has thus been identified with the help of concepts in philosophy.

In keeping with our basic approach to Jainism *not* as an autonomous tradition, but as an integral aspect of Indian thought, we commenced our disquisition with a reference to the general Indian concept of *darśana* as providing the nearest equivalent of *philosophy*. The presupposition clearly was that the concept of *darśana* is indicative not merely of areas of overlap between western and Indian approaches to philosophy but also of the distinctive features of the latter. The implication further was that a reference to the Indian viewpoint (and the Jaina perspective as reflective of it) should not be understood as pointing to a totally different approach.

In fact the importance accorded to the latter idea has been highlighted in this study by explicitly considering those ideas which are usually recounted as the hallmarks of a *philosophic approach*, — the ideas of empirical observation, rational analysis and "system-building". To express the idea slightly differently, the passage of thought has been from the familiar to the unfamiliar in the world of philosophy. Starting with the well-known ideas regarding philosophy as is understood in the west, we went into an exploration of the not so well-known aspects of the Indian approach as reflected in the Jaina tradition.

It needs to be reiterated here that our reference to the western idea of philosophy even while considering a specific viewpoint within the Indian tradition was born out of the consideration that *philosophy* is a western word, rather than looking upon the western idea as providing a model for philosophising. Furthermore, the fact that the tradition of philosophy in India has had a parallel existence (though not a parallel pattern of growth) would signify that understanding the Indian conception of philosophy (of which the Jaina view represents an inextricable strand) entails a comprehension of aspects of it which stand out distinctly in addition to those which are comparable. It was for this reason that the concept of *darśana* was subjected to a three-fold analysis as a prelude to delineating the Jaina view. The idea of philosophy as being critically directed toward evaluating the claims of reason was pointed out as a distinctive characteristic in this regard.

Our suggestion was that Jainism as metaphilosophy is easily discernible from the idea of criticism implicit in the concept of *darśana*. As such, the Jaina view may be visualised as an explicit articulation of the need for criticism in philosophy. All the same, no rigid dichotomy between the subject-matter and methods of critical inquiry even would be warranted, we maintained.

The idea of the complex Real as the subject-matter of philosophy espoused in the Jaina tradition was then proposed as the basis of the contention that a comprehensive understanding of the nature of Reality would preclude the stance of thwarting creative possibilties since the complex nature of Reality emerges from taking into account the objective as well as the subjective aspects and conceding that an in-depth analysis of both aspects reveals even more clearly the variegated nature of Reality, varying approaches to it and the resulting multifacted picture which needs recognition in the first place. Secondly, and in fact arising out of such recognition, the methods of approach need to be accorded importance and significance in such a way that full play is given to the process of reasoning.

Epistemologically considered, the importance accorded to reasoning as a method in philosophy can itself be viewed as being responsible for the Jaina philosphers' systematically analysing the processes of knowing. For, a comprehensive understanding of Reality, by definition, entails the usage of reason for visualising *how* the varied aspects of Reality could be apprehended. Such an analysis is itself a pointer to reasoning as an important tool in philosophy; add to it the elaborate consideration of inference as well as the full-fledged syllogistic argument proposed, the vital role of logic in philosophising would come to the fore.

In a number of other ways too, the crucial significance accorded to logic can be illustrated. The most important of these is the query raised about the efficacy of reason to fully comprehend the nature of Reality, notwithstanding the recognition accorded to it. Here again the complex nature of Reality recognised by reason seems to suggest that the faculty of reasoning too cannot be considered ultimately efficacious in reaching out to its goal. Though the goal of reasoning may be postulated as nothing less than a complete comprehension of Reality, the self-critical capacity that the power of reasoning engenders, results in a clear recognition of its inability to be equal to the task. The usage of reason may then be said to have resulted in pointing to the limitations of it.

This is suggestive of two things : one,. that Reality needs a trans-rational method of comprehension and two, a system of philosophy asserting itslef to be the only valid one which has seized truth fully becomes suspect. In the light of the analysis of Jainism as a system of philosophy, it has been noted that like the rest of the Indian tradition, Jainism accepts whole-heartedly the need to transcend the realm of reasoning and thus postulates that intuitive experience could be considered ultimately effective in comprehending the nature of Reality. It needs to be reiterated that transcending the plane of reasoning signifies that philosophy is considered here as supra-rational and not as infra-rational. The importance of reasoning as a method in philosophy is fully conceded, though the limitations of the method are recognised too. Our interpretation of the tradition as meta-philosophy has pointed to the critical stance it takes of systems of philosophy which do not accept even the relative validity of the contributions made by rival schools of thought.

The two aspects of the Jaina approach to philosophy referred to just now are, it is obvious, closely related, —the first suggesting, as a logical sequel, the second in which the critical approach adopted towards the very process of system-building is quite apparent. We have maintained that two celebrated theories, *Nayavāda* and *Syādvāda* in the Jaina tradition, are specifically indicative of the meta-philosophical approach characterising the whole tradition.

By considering them both as aspects of *Anekāntavāda, the Doctrine of Manifoldness of Reality, we have already indicated that the base-argument of Jainism as meta-philosophy* is the undeniable fact of the existence of many rival schools of thought. The statement may seem to be a truism, but a careful consideration of it would indicate how the Jaina view of the need for criticism in philosophy is arrived at by asking a fundamental question which is generally glossed over. The Jaina philosopher seems to maintain that a philosopher has the important task of raising the question: "Why, in the first place, are there divergent schools of philosophy characterised by a feeling of animosity and an attitude of rivalry rather than by a sense of belonging as partners in a joint-venture, viz. philosophising ?"

This is a basic issue to which a philosopher should address himself; for the fact of *diversity of philosophical positions* needs to be *explained* and not tacitly accepted as inevitable. The Jaina philosophers' serious concern with this problem stems from the consideration that if the 'fact' is accepted without questioning, the diverse schools will be seen only as different from and *opposed to* each other, whereas a deliberate analysis of the situation (of rival systems of thought vying with each other for honours) would reveal a deeper dimension which holds within it a common core paradoxically engendering different approaches.

The common core, in terms of the technical details delineated by *Anekāntavāda*, incorporates within itself, the attempts of different inquiring minds at unraveling the complex characteristic of Reality. In our review of the meta-philosophical significance of the doctrine of *Anekānta*, it has already been indicated that the idea of complexity of Reality which is only implicitly evident from the fact of many (*aneka*) theories being available, is explicated by considering the idea of manifoldness (*anekānta*).

It remains here to reiterate that some of the seminal metaphysical problems (like the Doctrine of Substance and Attribute, Universals and Particulars) which come to be considered for substantiating the idea of manifoldness, *are not* peculiar either to Jainism or to Indian philosophy in general, but are important ones in the history of western philosophy as well. The divergent viewpoints taken on these issues during the centuries of philosphising in the West—starting from the pre-Socratic era and continuing upto present times—would also show that the same problem (of understanding Reality) has been analysed differently by different schools and that they together point to the common core of concern, the manifold aspects of the problem under investigation. In this way the idea of *perspectives* comes to the fore. A slight digression here to refer to a parallel idea in Bertrand Russell's thought would be quite appropriate for considering the deeper significance of the Jaina view of *Anekānta*.

To explain his theory that the physical object perceived (and thence also the external world in general) is a *logical construction*, Russell proposes his theory of sense data. His argument in brief is this. Since different sets of sense data are presented to different people, different perceptions of objects result and, correspondingly, different pictures of the external world emerge. The differences are attributable to at least two factors: one, different minds being associated with different bodies; and two, the different places from which the objects are looked at. In regard to the first, it should be noted that owing to the varied types of association of minds and bodies, each mind apprehends the world from a standpoint peculiar to itself. In regard to the second, it should be stated that the existence of a number of worlds corresponding to the differences between places from which the world is looked at, has to be accepted. Thus an infinite number of worlds corresponding to the infinite number of minds at work and the infinite number of places from which a view is had, can be postulated. Whether any mind is actually perceiving or not and similarly whether any of the places from which the world is looked at are actually occupied or not, it can still be maintained that an infinite number of views of the world *are* possible.

But even when we confine our attention to the actual observers and to the specific places from which the world is looked at, it cannot be gainsaid that different views are got. These are referred to as *perspectives* by Russell and he maintain that the different perspectives can be explained by sets of sense data which are peculiar to them. Thus, an aspect of the world (which is perceived from a particular perspective) is regarded by him as a member of the system of aspects which *is* the world. The aspect which is immediately perceived is a set of sense data and the world which is the system of all the different sense data apprehended through all possible perspectives, is a logical construction.

In terms of Russell's doctrine of perspectives explained above, the Jaina theory pf *Anekānta* can well be visualised as suggesting that the very *possibility* of divergent perspectives would indicate that a categorical assertion on behalf of *any* viewpoint taken, would itself render it a subject for critical scrutiny. If various viewpoints *are* possible, how can it be stated categorically that one view *alone* is to be accepted as valid and all others rejected outright as untenable? Thus it is that *Anekāntavāda* lays the emphasis on the meta-philosophical function of philosophy. This aspect of the work of philosophy is termed its critical function.

As we have explained, the critical function is not aimed at putting down systems of thought which have been deligently built nor condemning them for taking the standpoints that they do. It is rather aimed at bringing in the necessary corrective to all one-sided views. Categorically maintaining the validity of any viewpoint *as against all others*, deserves to be described as taking a one-sided view, and applying a corrective would signify espousing the need to be non-one-sided. This in turn points to turning away from the habit of outright rejection of theories on the count that one theory alone is wholly acceptable.

It is worth recounting that the *Anekānta* view, in this sense, it *not* born out of strategic consideratins but out of the recognition that comprehending Reaity involves that theories need to be analysed not with a view to merely identifying their pitfalls but with a view to finding out which of their aspects deserve to be retained in the overall attempt at arriving at a synoptic view. The procedures of *analysis* as well as *synthesis* are thus considered equally valuable in the constructive-critical role to be played by philosophy.

By reviewing and reinterpreting the idea of perspectives, we have already considered in effect, the significance of *Nayavāda* as the analytical aspect of the Jaina view of the critical function of philosophy proposed in *Anekāntavāda.* We shall adopt a similar procedure in regard to *Syādvāda* to highlight the synthetic aspect constituting the other component of critical philosophy.

By prefixing the *syāt*-particle to every proposition regarding Reality, the Jaina philosophers scrupulously avoid the tone of categoricalness in regard to the various views proposed. The prefix is also indicative of the possibility of arriving at a synthesis. for, in the absence of the prefix, several categorical positions,—different from and even opposed to each other —would have to be considered equally and absolutely valid. And this, even on the face of it, would indicate irreconcilability ad internal contradiction and consequently would not even hold out bleak prospects of seeing their relatedness. The prefixing of the seven propositions in the celebrated formulation of the *Syādvāda* (elaborated in the previous chapter) then is *not* to be understood as casting doubts in regard to all the views which have been put forward but as a *critical approach* to absolutistic claims of each of them. It seems to me that the Jaina philosophers also imply that if the claims of complete validity from the various schools are allowed to be entertained, the question as to which one of them is to be accepted and which others are to be rejected, would logically arise and hence, even to start with, only a qualified acceptance (and obviously too, only a qualified rejection) of the claims to validity is suggested as a way of resolving the problem of understanding Reality.

It would thus become clear that the significance of *Syādvāda* as a criticism of forthright formulations of philosophical doctrines consists in its holding out hopes that the situation in the world of philosophy is not as hopeless as its seems to be. Despite differing formulations and varying types of emphasis laid by schools of thought, it is still possible that valuable insights into the nature of Reality can be gained from the various views held,—this by adopting the procedure of constructive criticism, by adopting the attitude that while rejection of absolute claims might be inevitable, acceptance of aspects of the theories is quite possible.

Such an interpretation of the significance of *Syādvāda* would also imply further that it truly makes for a balancing effect in so far as it complements the function of *Nayavāda* which is aimed at a critical evaluation of all one-sided views. For, the rejection of extreme views (which the doctrine of *Nayavāda* basically stands for) is mainly aimed at pointing to the need for moderate formulations which would be acceptable. Since both aspects of the idea of criticism as synthesis (found in *Syādvāda*) and the idea of criticism as analysis (found in *Nayavāda*) have already been explained in this study, suffice it to reiterate here as a concluding note that the Jaina view of the meta-philosophical function of philosophy consists not simply in sitting in judgment over the question: Which school of philosophy is to be accepted and which others are to be rejected? but rather in evaluating objectively the claims and counter-claims put forward by different systems and identifying the contributions they *all* have made in the difficult enterprise called *philosophising* which is common to them all.

BIBLIOGRAPHY

Acārāṅga-Sūtra

Āvaśyakaniryukti

Bhagavatī-Sūtra

Chakravarti, A. *Religion of Ahimsa*, Bombay : Ratanchand Hirachand, 1957.

Chatterjee, Satischandra. & Datta, Direndramohan. *An Introduction To Indian Philosophy*, Calcutta : University of Calcutta, 1968 (first published, 1939)

Coward, Harold. G. edt., *Studies in Indian Thought*, Delhi : Motilal Banarsidass, 1983

Daśavaikālikaniryukti

Dasgupta, S.N. A *History of Indian Philosophy*, Vol. I, Cambridge : Cambridge university Press, 1963 (first published, 1922)

Datta, D.M. *Philosophical Perspectives*, Patna : Bharati Bhawan, 1972

De Bury, Wm Theodore. edt., *Sources of Indian Tradition*, New York: Columbia University Press, 1958

Dixit, K.K. *Jaina Ontology*, Ahmedabad : L.D. Institute of Indology, 1971

Dravya-Saṅgraha

Gopalan, S. *Outlines of Jainism*, New Delhi : Wiley Eastern Pvt. Ltd., 1973

Hiriyanna, M. *Outlines of Indian Philosophy*, London : George Allen & Unwin Ltd., 1931

Matilal, B.K. *The Central Philosophy of Jainism*, Ahmedabad : L.D. Institute of Indology, 1981

Mehta, M.L. *Outlines of Jaina Philosophy*, Bangalore : Jain Mission Society, 1954

Mookerjee, Satkari. *The Jaina Philosophy of Non- Absolutism*, Calcutta : Bharati Mahavidyalaya Publications, 1944

Murty, K. Satchidananda. *Philosophy in India*, Delhi : Motilal Banarsidas, 1985

Naya-karṇikā

Nyāya-Kumuda-candra

Padmarajiah, Y.J. *Jaina Theories of Reality and Knowledge*, Bombay: Jain Sahitya Vikas Mandal, 1963

Pancāsti-kāya

Pappu, S.S. Rama Rao and Puligandla, R. edt., *Indian Philosophy Past and Future*, Delhi : Motilal Banarsidass, 1982

Pramāṇa-mīmāmsa

Pramāṇanaya-tattvālokālaṅkāra

Pravacanasāra

Radhakrishnan, S., *Indian Philosophy*, Vol. I, London : George Allen & Unwin Ltd., 1942

_______________ *An Idealist View of Life*, London : George Allen & Unwin Ltd.,, 1932

Sanmatī-tarka

Sarvārtha-siddhi

Smith, Wilfred Cantwell., *The Meaning and End of Religion*, New York: The New American Library of World Literature, 1964

Sūtrakṛtāṅga

Syādvādaratnākara

Syādvādamañjarī

Tatia, N. *Studies in Jaina Philosophy*, Banaras : Jain Cultural Research Society, 1951

Tattvārtha-bhāṣya

Tattvārtha-śloka-vārttika

Tattvārtha-sūtra

Vidyabhusana, Satis Chandra. *A History of Indian Logic*, Delhi : Motilal Banarsidass, 1978 (first published, 1970)

INDEX